What is her role in an in
ities be? How should a l<
necessary—or is it? Wh
shines the clear light or

Since Christ loved the church enough to die for her, every believer ought
to share that passion. Jeffrey Johnson clearly does, and I believe you will
find his enthusiasm contagious.

—John MacArthur

Jeffrey Johnson has written a book on the church that is short enough to
read right now, clear enough to be understood, and important enough to
help many of us follow Jesus Christ as He intended—as members of His
church. Why not read it now?

—Mark Dever

Like the apostle Paul before him, Jeffrey Johnson demonstrates that he is
jealous for Christ's church with a godly jealousy and that his one great desire is to present her to Christ as a pure virgin (II Corinthians 11:2). Like a
caring and discerning physician, he has not only correctly diagnosed what
ails the contemporary evangelical church but he has also prescribed the
proper cure—a sincere and persistent adherence to the doctrine of Sola
Scriptura. This concise yet thorough work should be required reading for
every pastor, congregation, and aspirant to the ministry.

—Paul Washer

In a day where many worship at the altar of pragmatism, the church is in
dire need of a biblical view of herself and her purpose. Pastor Jeffrey Johnson offers a concise, sobering, and eye-opening message for a generation
in need of ecclesiological reformation. Johnson addresses the issues we
face today and roots them in their historical/theological context. Jeffrey
reminds us that the deep, abiding truths of Scripture are sufficient to sus-
tain the bride of Christ in every age.

—Voddie Baucham Jr.

Like a carpenter refinishing a classic piece of furniture, Jeffrey Johnson strips away layers of human tradition and worldly-wise philosophy to restore our view of the church to its biblical simplicity. In this book the church shines! Johnson offers basic teaching on the purposes, worship, membership, and leadership of the church from a Baptist perspective. As a Reformed Christian I found especially valuable his emphasis on the holiness of the church and its worship as ordained by God's holy Word and lived out in His holy presence.

—Joel R. Beeke

Here is a book which every member of every Baptist church (and even some other denominations) needs to read and apply to their churches and their lives. The book is very brief and direct and even applicable and necessary, especially for our day. The book covers almost every aspect of what a church is and what it should and should not be doing, according to the Scriptures.

—Richard P. Belcher Sr.

Jeffrey Johnson provides a big picture view of what the church is about without clutter or confusion. In understandable, straight-forward chapters, the nature and practice of church life is explained so that even the newest of believers may comprehend. He has not tried to be innovative but faithful to the Bible in his presentation. Among its uses, try it with those who are new to church life and need an explanation in lucid, accessible language.

—Jim Elliff

This book of Jeffrey Johnson's has a loving and exalted view of the church of Jesus Christ, but it is also aware of its tensions and imperfections as congregations are having to live in a fallen world under the holy requirements of the head of the church. This book will help you to understand the life of the church, its duties and blessings, and it will encourage you to give your years to serving and strengthening the people of God.

—Geoff Thomas

There are two resounding features that stand forth in this book: doctrinal clarity and practical instruction. The local church is the only God-instituted context for believers to live out their lives in Christ, yet many Christians remain unaware of what the local church is and how God has determined for it to function. Without question, this book is an immensely helpful asset for the church in our day.

—**Anthony Mathenia**

With refreshing vigour and stimulating simplicity, Jeffrey Johnson gives us a sinewy outline of Scriptural principles for the nature and life of Christ's church. It is brief enough to be a useful introduction but deep enough to prompt careful thought and promote earnest practice. This little book is a fine antidote to shallow, casual, lukewarm attitudes to God's household, putting in place a legitimately high conception of the people of the living God working out their holy purposes in the presence of the living God.

—**Jeremy Walker**

The idea of church membership today is either an assumption that has never been challenged or considered biblically or else abandoned by new church starts as a useless relic of the past that is irrelevant for churches and Christians now. We can be thankful that there are pastors such as Jeffrey Johnson who address this issue from a biblical perspective and demonstrate the importance of meaningful membership in a local church by Christians today.

—**Don Whitney**

The
Church

Her Nature, Authority, Purpose, and Worship

The
Church

Her Nature, Authority, Purpose, and Worship

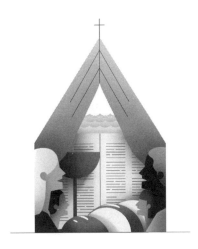

Jeffrey D. Johnson

mediagratiae

The Church:
Her Nature, Authority, Purpose, and Worship

Copyright © 2020 by Jeffrey D. Johnson
Cover design by Ordinary Folk
Printed in the United States
Published by Media Gratiae
PO Box 21
New Albany, MS 38652

ISBN 978-0-9886681-9-5

Dedicated to

Greg and Ingrid Stevens

Contents

Introduction

A CHURCH'S VIEW OF GOD, man, and salvation has a vital impact on its practices. Theology proper (the doctrine of God), anthropology (the doctrine of man), soteriology (the doctrine of salvation), and ecclesiology (the doctrine of the church) should never be separated in practice. What we believe about God, man, and salvation will consequently influence the way we do church. Having a high view of God and a low view of man, or a low view of God and a high view of man, will determine whether a church is God centered (theocentric) or man centered (anthropocentric). In the end, the church's view of God, man, and salvation will reveal whom the church is seeking to please.

Practically speaking, there are two views of salvation within evangelical Protestantism: (1) Easy-believism and (2) Lordship salvation.

Easy-believism

Easy-believism is the most widely accepted view of salvation, evidenced in the way most churches conduct themselves. What is easy-believism? It is a watered-down view of salvation that comes from a low view of God and a high view of man. The notion is that repentance is not necessary for salvation and all that is required by God is a simple decision to "accept Jesus into your heart." The opinion is that sinners are capable, within themselves, of making this choice; all they need is a good pitchman (i.e., preacher) to show them the advantages of heaven in comparison to the alternative.

With this low view of God comes the idea that He does not demand any more from us than a simple prayer, often accomplished by repeating the words of the pastor after walking to the front of the church. At best, the preacher may remind us at the last second that we must repeat "the sinner's prayer" from "the heart."

To demand more from the sinner than a simple prayer is deemed unnecessary and a hindrance to persuading many to respond. For instance, the manner in which the Lord handled the rich young ruler—when He told him to forsake his idol (his true god) by giving all his money away—is not a method of evangelism conducive to producing a lot of converts.

With this low view of salvation comes the opinion that we do not need to make any major sacrifices to gain heaven; we can be saved and continue to live our lives as before. It is therefore seen as completely unnecessary to forsake all, including our lives, to follow the Lord. All that is believed to be required to go to heaven is to "add" Jesus to our lives. See how easy salvation is? Escape hell, stay in control of your life, and receive a ticket to heaven by a simple prayer that includes the heartfelt words, "I accept Jesus into my heart." Following this method of evangelism, there would have been no need for the rich young ruler to be disappointed; he could have had Christ and retained his riches.

Easy-believism leads to another dangerous doctrine known as *carnal Christianity*. Since salvation does not demand self-denial and submission to Christ as Lord, all who have repeated the sinner's prayer must be saved no matter how they live their lives. Under this delusion, drunkards, adulterers, and idolaters are preached into heaven at their funeral because they said a prayer when they were a child, and to be a Christian, love for God and a love for God's people (the church) is optional. Churches are full of people who have recited the sinner's prayer; thus, it is assumed that most churchgoers are true Christians.

With a cheap view of salvation, it is easy to see why many churches operate the way they do: as businesses. The church wants to grow as rapidly as possible, and the unconverted want a clear conscience as cheaply as possible; thus, the church is willing to sell out the gospel by offering customers an affordable salvation. The important thing is to get people into the doors of the church, by any means possible, then get them saved. To keep these people coming back, the church must continue to give them what they want: a smooth conscience. This is obtained by a little bit of biblical truth, a touch of conviction, and a whole lot of entertainment.

The *consumer-driven* church wants to know how to attract and satisfy the most people. How can the church keep such seekers, like the rich young ruler who sought the Lord but unfortunately went away sorrowful, from leaving disappointed? In an attempt to be sensitive to them, the church has gone from taking its direction from the Scriptures to consulting marketing firms and employing the business tactics of the world. It has turned to *pragmatism,* where the end justifies the means. In other words, the church feels satisfied that the Lord's blessing is upon its efforts because of rapid growth and record-breaking attendance.

With this businesslike approach, moralistic, therapeutic deism has taken hold of churches. The church has switched from being an assembly of saints who worship God in spirit and truth to a social gathering of nominal Christians who hear weekly motivational speeches about how staying positive and doing what's right allows them to experience their "best life now." God's glory and personal holiness are no longer the driving forces behind the activities and functions of the church; rather, what governs the church is the desire to keep people happy as they live a life without completely submitting to the lordship of Christ.

In the end, a low view of God and a high view of man leads to easy-believism and man-centered churches that operate like consumer-driven businesses.

Lordship Salvation

Churches with a high view of God and a low view of man have a different perspective on salvation and, thus, a different perspective on the purpose and functions of the church. This understanding specifically affects how such a church views salvation: not principally for the sake of man but for the glory of God. That is, the problem is not that sinners are going to hell but that sinners do not glorify the Lord in their lives. This perspective may sound like a minor concern, but it ultimately determines if a church is man centered or God centered.

If salvation is ultimately for God's glory, then it should not be perceived as merely obtaining a free ticket to heaven. Rather, salvation delivers sinners from their sin, both its penalty and power. This is the very reason Christ came—to save His people from their sins (Matt. 1:21). Sin and the cause of sin (depravity) are man's greatest problems. Sin is the reason people go to hell and are under the wrath of God in the first place. And what is sin? Sin is any thought or action that comes short of the glory of God (Rom. 3:23). Thus, salvation delivers man from sin, the very thing that robs God of His glory.

Salvation delivers us from the guilt of sin in *justification*, and it delivers us from the power of sin in *regeneration* and *sanctification*. Those who are saved do go to heaven but only because they are saved from the guilt and power of sin.

More importantly, salvation reconciles God and sinners together through Christ Jesus. Sin has separated us from God, and Christ Jesus, the perfect Lamb of God, is the only way to the Father (John 14:6).

If Christ came to save His people from the guilt and power of sin to a reconciled relationship with God, then salvation is only for those who are seeking to be freed from sin and desiring a personal relationship with God. Therefore, if there is no repentance, there is no salvation. To cling to any one sin or to love anything more than Christ, as the rich young ruler clung to his wealth, is an act of rebellion against Christ. As long as we remain rebellious, we remain unrepentant. Without repentance, we are not seeking to be reconciled to God.

This is why the Lord said, "For I came not to call the righteous, but sinners" to repentance (Matt. 9:13). He also claimed, "If anyone would come after me, let him deny himself and take up his cross and follow me" (Matt. 16:24), and "Any one of you who does not renounce all that he has cannot be my disciple" (Luke 14:33).

The argument against lordship salvation is that it seems to make salvation dependent on something more than faith in Christ Jesus. If we must submit to Christ as Lord, then this means that salvation is by faith *plus* submission. This cannot be, so they say, because salvation is by faith alone; to demand that we submit to Christ for salvation is to require something in addition to faith. Faith is believing, and all that is needed for salvation is for us to believe that Jesus existed and died on the cross for our sins. Salvation is supposed to be that simple. Let us get people to confess that Jesus is their Savior first, and then we can work on getting them to submit to Him as Lord later, so the reasoning goes.

Salvation *is* by faith alone. But salvation is only for those who know they are lost. As the Lord said, "For the Son of Man came to seek and to save the lost" (Luke 19:10) and "Those who are well have no need of a physician, but those who are sick. . . . For I came not to call the righteous, but sinners" (Matt. 9:12–13).

Man's greatest need is to know that he has a need. In other words, if we are unaware that we are sinners, then obviously, we will not see that we need a Savior. If salvation is principally viewed as getting a ticket to heaven, then all that is necessary for us to want salvation is a desire to escape the flames of hell. But if salvation is deliverance and freedom from sin and reconciliation with God through Christ Jesus, it is necessary that we realize we are sinners first, then have a desire to be delivered from our sins. If we are not sorry for our rebellious acts, we do not want to be saved from them. If we don't want forgiveness and freedom from the power of sin (as evidenced by a willingness to forsake everything, even our lives), then we don't want the salvation that Christ offers in the gospel.

What are we to do after we see ourselves as guilty before God? What are we to do when we are troubled and remorseful for sinning against God? What are we to do when we acknowledge our need for Christ and want to follow Him? What are we to do if we desire to be saved from our sins? The answer is simple—*believe* in the Lord Jesus Christ.

We are not to trust in our righteousness but, instead, to look to Christ for forgiveness and deliverance from the grip of sin. We must believe the glorious gospel—that Christ, who was without sin, died for our sins so that we might be justified before God in the Beloved.

Faith alone saves us, but for us to be in a state of mind where we desire salvation, we must first come to the end of ourselves. We must realize we are sinners and are unable to justify ourselves before God by our righteousness.

Thus, by repentance, we acknowledge our guilt and remorsefully turn from our sins to Christ for forgiveness. By faith, we look to Christ for forgiveness, where we are assured that He has paid it all. This is why the Lord said, "Repent and believe in the gospel" (Mark 1:15).

Technically speaking, repentance and faith cannot be chronologically separated. John Murray clarifies this:

> The interdependence of faith and repentance can be readily seen when we remember that faith is faith in Christ for salvation

from sin. But if faith is directed to salvation from sin, there must be hatred of sin and the desire to be saved from it. Such hatred of sin involves repentance which essentially consists in turning from sin to God. Again, if we remember that repentance is turning from sin unto God, the turning to God implies faith in the mercy of God as revealed in Christ. It is impossible to disentangle faith and repentance.[1]

With a low view of salvation and a high view of man, it is natural to think a little pressure and persuasion is all that is needed for people to be talked into accepting Christ. If all sinners need to do is believe in a Jesus who wants to give them a free ticket to heaven, then it's no wonder that churches can baptize so many.

On the other hand, if a church has a high view of salvation and a low view of man, everything changes. Those who are enslaved to sin may be able to confess that Jesus died on the cross for their sins, but apart from the work of the Holy Spirit, they will be unable and unwilling to forsake their sins. Sinners, by their very nature, will always love themselves more than they love God. Sinners are enslaved to both their selfish will and to the devil (Eph. 2:1–3), which makes it humanly impossible for them to love God enough to forsake all for Christ willingly.

To have a love for God and make certain sacrifices is one thing, but to love God above all things is quite another. To desire a Christ who wants to give people their "best life now" seems reasonable enough for most churchgoers, but to desire a Christ who requires sinners to forsake all, even their lives, seems entirely unreasonable. And it may be easy to talk someone into repeating a prayer, especially with high-pressure tactics and emotional music playing quietly in the background, but to awaken a sinner to feel true remorse for offending God and cause them to be willing to give up their life is impossible.

---

1   John Murray, *Redemption Accomplished and Applied* (Grand Rapids: Eerdmans, 1955), 113.

After the disciples had heard the Lord explain the high cost of discipleship to the rich young ruler, they turned and asked the Lord, "Who then can be saved?" The Lord responded by saying, "With man this is impossible" (Matt. 19:25–26).

How are sinners saved then? Sinners are saved by grace alone. Thankfully, after the Lord said, "With man this is impossible," He went on to say, "but with God all things are possible" (v. 26).

How does God save sinners? The Holy Spirit regenerates their hearts so they can willingly believe the gospel (John 3:5–8), for it is the gospel that is "the power of God for salvation to everyone who believes" (Rom. 1:16). Without the saving power of the Holy Spirit, sinners would have remained dead in their trespasses and sins. Only God can change hearts of stone and bring rebellious sinners to repentance and faith in Christ Jesus. "For by grace you have been saved through faith. And this is not your own doing; it is the gift of God" (Eph. 2:8). Though God uses, even commands, His people to evangelize the lost, it is only He who can bring people to faith in Christ Jesus and, thus, grow the church (1 Cor. 3:6).

Adhering to this view of God, man, and salvation changes everything about the church. If it is impossible to change the hearts of sinners by mere persuasion or through the manipulation of the emotions, and if it is impossible for sinners to deny themselves and submit to Christ as Lord without the illuminating grace of the Holy Spirit, then the church should focus on proclaiming the truth—the one thing the Holy Spirit has chosen to use to save and sanctify sinners.

The church will not be judged by the number of baptisms or on the size of its membership but on how faithful it has been in teaching the whole counsel of God. Yes, the church needs to have a deep passion for lost souls and should seek to reach them for the glory of God. But the church needs to remember that the best thing it can do for lost souls is to preach an uncompromised gospel, one that calls sinners to repent of their sins and be reconciled to God by faith in Christ Jesus.

The church should desire to grow *numerically* but not at the cost of growing *spiritually*. As John Owen reminds us, "The great business of the church is not our number by addition, but by grace, by growing up in Christ."[2] Marketing, gimmicks, and entertainment may build a large congregation, but only the truth of God's Word will build the church and purify its membership for the glory of God.

The core conviction behind this book is based on a high view of God and a low view of man, because the church stands or falls on the right view of God, man, and salvation. Where there is no gospel, there is no church! If we want to know if a particular church carries the approval of God and is fulfilling its mission, then we must look to see how the church is handling and proclaiming the gospel of Jesus Christ.

A proper view of God, man, and salvation has many ramifications on how a church functions. What is the principal purpose of the church? What does it mean for a church to be holy? What are the qualifications and responsibilities of church membership? How does the church handle church discipline? The answers to these questions are born out of a biblical view of God, man, and salvation. The goal of this book is to show how a high view of God and a low view of man should shape our understanding of the nature, authority, purpose, and worship of the local church.

---

2 John Owen, "The Mutual Care of Believers Over One Another," in *The Works of John Owen* (Edinburgh: Banner of Truth, 1965), 16:477–78.

Part 1

The Nature
of the Church

So then you are no longer strangers and aliens, but
you are fellow citizens with the saints and members
of the household of God, built on the foundation of
the apostles and prophets, Christ Jesus himself being
the cornerstone, in whom the whole structure, being
joined together, grows into a holy temple in the Lord.
In him you also are being built together into a dwelling
place for God by the Spirit.

Ephesians 2:19–22

The Marks
of the Church

WHAT IS THE CHURCH? Are Christians required to join themselves to a local church? What are the privileges and responsibilities of church membership? What is the authority of the church? What is church discipline, and how is the church to be governed? What is the purpose of the church? What are the activities of the church? How should the church express its worship? The answers to these important questions should not be left to one's opinion or their pragmatic or relativistic ideas but yielded from the sure foundation of God's written Word. The purpose of this study, therefore, is to establish what the Bible teaches about the nature, authority, purpose, and worship of the local church.

Before we can properly understand the authority, purpose, and worship of the church, we need to know the nature of the church. In other words, what is "the church"? There is a lot of confusion about how to answer this question. We often think of centers of worship as churches. Yet not once does the Bible speak of the church as a physical building. Chapels, cathedrals, basilicas, and sanctuaries may help facilitate the functions and worship of the church, but they are not the church. Rather, as we will seek to explain in this first chapter, three essential marks define the church—*unity*, *purity*, and *verity*.

1. The Church Is God's Unified Communion

The Lord Jesus, in Matthew 16:18, was the first to use the word *church* to describe His people when He said, "I will build my church, and the gates of hell shall not prevail against it." The Greek word translated as *church* is *ekklesia*, which means "assembly" (see Acts 19:32, 41). Yet when Christ used the word *ekklesia* to speak about His people, He elevated the word to mean more than just an ordinary assembly of people. He elevated the word to mean the particular gathering of people that He would personally build. Though some may "plant" the gospel by evangelizing unbelievers, and others may "water" the gospel through teaching believers, it is only God who can give the "increase" (1 Cor. 3:6–7). That is to say, it is the Lord, and only the Lord, who adds to the church daily those who are being saved (Acts 2:47).

Consequently, because Christ is the one who builds the church, Christ is the one who *owns* the church. Christ said, "I will build *my* church" (Matt. 16:18, emphasis added). This means that the church does not belong to the elders or to the people but to the Lord. This is crucial to understand. Christ is the sole proprietor of the church. The word *church* communicates this truth. The English word *church* is derived from the Greek word *kuriakon,* the neuter adjective of *kurios*, which is translated *Lord*. The word *kuriakon* is only found twice in the New Testament and means "belonging to the Lord" (see 1 Cor. 11:20; Rev. 1:10).

One of the identifying characteristics of the church is that it *belongs* to the Lord. That is, the thing that distinguishes the church from secular societies, social clubs, and other religious congregations is that the church is the unique possession of God.

This is why it is common to find the phrases *church of God* and *church of Christ* repeatedly in the New Testament. Consequently, the church of God, as it is defined in the Bible, is not a group of unbelievers who assemble in the name of Christ, such as Mormons and Jehovah Witnesses, but rather it consists of His people—those particular people who have been called out by God through personal faith in Christ.

The material God uses to build His church is His redeemed people (Eph. 2:19–22). Peter explains that the saints are the "living stones" that make up a "spiritual house" (1 Peter 2:5). The cornerstone is Christ, with the other foundation stones consisting of the prophets and apostles (Eph. 2:20). All these building blocks, moreover, are being laid and interwoven together to make up a *single* structure or temple.

The church is likened not only to a building or a temple but also to a body (Eph. 1:22–23). Like the metaphor of a building, the metaphor of the body communicates that the church consists of different members who are united to form a single entity. In that, the church has multiple members (1 Cor. 12:14) who are spiritually united and interlocked into *one* spiritual body under the single headship of Christ Jesus (Col. 1:18–19). Thus, the church is one (Eph. 2:14).

The Invisible Unity of the Universal Church

Yet, it is important to note that the unity of the church is not due to some external organization. Rather, the unity of the mystical body of Christ is a by-product of the communion and union that all believers share in the person of Christ by faith. This union with Christ is not physical or visible but invisible and spiritual.

In other words, believers are *not* united to Christ by joining a local church. Rather, they are united to Christ by faith, and afterward, they are inwardly compelled by the Spirit and the Word to join a local church. In this way, only believers are members of the universal church, and only members of the universal church are proper candidates for local church membership.

Only when we are spiritually united to Christ by faith are we united to the invisible and universal body of Christ. Consequently, there is one invisible and universal body of Christ (Eph. 4:4), which is entered into by being spiritually and personally united to Christ, the head of the church, through faith (Gal. 2:20). As John Calvin stated:

> The church is called "catholic," or "universal," because there could not be two or three churches unless Christ be torn asunder—which cannot happen! But all the elect are so united in Christ that as they are dependent on one Head, they also grow together into one body, being joined and knit together as are the limbs of a body. They are made truly one since they live together in one faith, hope, and love, and in the same Spirit of God.[1]

Faith has not only united us with Christ but with all those who also are united to Christ. This union makes us "one body in Christ, and individually members one of another" (Rom. 12:5). In the body of Christ, there is no division between Jew and Gentile, rich and poor, or male and female; we are all one in Christ Jesus (Gal. 3:28; Eph. 4:4). This oneness is not merely in identity but in the vitality of spiritual life.

Christ is the life of all who believe. The life that each believer has in Christ, however, is the very life that is mutually shared by all believers. This shared life binds every Christian together into one spiritual family. "Among the attributes of the church," according to Francis Turretin, "the first is its unity, which flows from its nature. For since it is a holy society and a mystical body, embracing all the elect united in the bond of the same spirit, faith and love with each other with Christ, it must necessarily have a certain unity by which

---

1 John Calvin, *Institutes of the Christian Religion*, ed. John T. McNeill, trans. Ford Lewis Battles (Philadelphia, PA: Westminster Press, 1977), 4.1.2.

all its members may be mutually joined together."[2] R. C. Sproul stated, "One of the most precious realities of the Christian faith is the unity that binds the hearts and souls of every Christian not only with Christ, but with each other."[3] Sproul explained that "though being in Christ is intensely personal and individual, it is never individualistic. Every individual who is personally united to Christ is at the same time personally united with every other person who is in Christ."[4] For this reason, James Bannerman, in his classic book on the church, stated: "The primary and normal idea of the church, as set forth in Scripture, is unquestionably that of a body of men spiritually united to Christ, and, in consequence of that union, one with each other, as they are one with Him."[5]

The Visible Unity of the Local Church

Because the church is made up of God's people who have been spiritually united, the individual members are called to assemble together (Heb. 10:25). This invisible and spiritual unity, as we shall see in chapter 3, inwardly constrains the united people of God to willfully and joyfully congregate into local assemblies.

Those who have fellowship and communion with Christ Jesus cannot help but have fellowship and communion with each other. It is the soul's invisible unity with the invisible Christ that compels believers who live in a physical body to outwardly unite in visible and local assemblies. The local church is simply an external expression of the internal unity that Christians have with each other in Christ Jesus.

It was for this reason that Christ used the word *assembly* (*ekklesia*) to describe His body (Col. 1:18). This word properly

---

2 Francis Turretin, *Institutes of Elenctic Theology*, 3:27.

3 R. C. Sproul, *Getting the Gospel Right: The Tie that Binds Evangelicals Together* (Grand Rapids: Baker, 1999), 23.

4 Sproul, 24.

5 James Bannerman, *The Church of Christ* (Edinburgh: Banner of Truth, 1974), 1:14.

describes the church because one of the defining marks of the church is that it consists of people who commune and fellowship in one place (1 Cor. 11:18; 14:23). All those whom God added to the church, for instance, continued to assemble together as "they devoted themselves to the apostles' teaching," to "fellowship, to the breaking of bread," and to prayer (Acts 2:42). For this reason, English Puritan Benjamin Keach claimed, "A church is a congregation of godly Christians, who as a stated assembly . . . do by mutual agreement and consent give themselves up to the Lord, and one another, according to the will of God; and do ordinarily meet together in one place."[6]

The saints meet together not only because God has united their hearts but because He has designed Christians to be interdependent. That is, they meet together because they cannot properly function without each other. God has purposefully gifted Christians differently and unequally so that they will need each other for their spiritual maturity. Though each member of the body of Christ receives their life and nourishment from the Head, they are individually designed to contribute to the spiritual growth of the whole body. As the apostle Paul explains: "From whom the whole body, joined and held together by every joint with which it is equipped, when each part is working properly, makes the body grow so that it builds itself up in love" (Eph. 4:16). Consequently, the church is a unified body is designed to grow, but only in sequence with the growth of its individual parts as they function together.

In other words, God designed the church in such a way that every member of the body is codependent. Somewhat like the inner working parts of a watch, every member is needed for the church to function properly. Each member of the body of Christ is needed for the mutual growth and edification of the whole. Just as "the eye cannot say to the hand, 'I have no need of you'" (1 Cor. 12:21),

---

6 Benjamin Keach, *The Glory of a True Church* (Conway, AR: Free Grace Press, 2016), 21.

Christians cannot say they have no need of one another. To go at it alone is like the foot severing itself from the rest of the body and thinking it can hop on to heaven by itself.

The members come together in local assemblies so the members can work and have fellowship and communion together. For this reason, the church is not just individual and unconnected saints; the church is *the communion of the saints*. As John Calvin remarked, "The communion of saints . . . expresses what the church is. It is as if one said that the saints are gathered into the society of Christ on the principle that whatever benefits God confers upon them, they should in turn share with one another."[7] Likewise, the Puritan William Dell summarized the nature of the church with these words:

> The church is the communion of the saints, which is the communion believers have with one another; not in the things of the world, or in the things of man, but in the things of God. For as believers have their union in the Son, and in the Father, so in them also they have their communion; and the communion they have with one another in God cannot be in their own things, but in things, even in his light, life, righteousness, wisdom, truth, love, power, peace, joy. This is the true communion of saints, and this communion of saints is the true Church of God.[8]

2. The Church Is a Holy Communion

The church is not only God's unified people, the church is God's sanctified people. This is the second essential mark of the church. In fact, the reason the saints are unified is that they have been sanctified in Christ Jesus. God's redeemed people have been sanctified in Christ Jesus by the truth of God's Word (1 Cor. 1:2).

---

7 Calvin, *Institutes*, 4.1.3.

8 William Dell, "The Way of True Peace and Unity in the True Church of Christ" in *Several Sermons and Discourses of William Dell* (London: Giles Calvert, 1652), 152.

God's people have been called out of the world of darkness and sin and translated into the kingdom of God's dear Son (Col. 1:13). They have been washed and sanctified by the blood of Jesus Christ (1 Cor. 6:11). Consequently, they are a holy nation and a kingdom of priests who have been consecrated by the Holy Spirit unto the Lord (1 Peter 2:5, 9).

The true church is holy by its very nature. As R. B. Kuiper stated, "Holiness is the very essence [of the church]. Holiness constitutes the church. The church is synonymous with holiness." Why does Kuiper associate holiness with the essence of the church? Because this is what the church is—holy. Kuiper went on to say, "[Holiness] is not just a mere armament that adds to its glory as a sparkling necklace may enhance the beauty of a fair woman. No, holiness is its very essence."[9]

The great business of the church, consequently, is to grow in unity and in holiness. It is sin that destroys unity, and thus God is seeking to bring His people into greater unity by delivering them from the bondage of sin and by sanctifying them by His truth (John 17:17).

3. The Church Is God's Truth-Bearing Communion

The church is "the pillar and ground of the truth" (1 Tim. 3:15 KJV). This means that the truth is not something that simply adorns the church but something that defines the very nature of the church. This is why *verity* is the third essential mark of the church.

First, the church is established on the truth. The foundation of the church is God's Word (Eph. 2:20). The church is built on the truth of Scripture. The church grows as people are united to the body of Christ by faith. Yet faith comes by hearing, and hearing

9 R. B. Kuiper, *The Glorious Body of Christ* (Edinburgh: Banner of Truth, 2001), 58.

comes by the Word of God (Rom. 10:17). In other words, without the Word, there is no salvation, and without salvation, there is no church.

Second, the church is governed by the truth. Christ is the head of the church (Col. 1:18), and Christ rules and directs His church through His Word (Matt. 28:20). Without the Bible, the church would be left to its own pragmatic strategies as it wandered around in the darkness to its own demise. Thankfully, the church has all it needs in the Scriptures to know and carry out its purposes (2 Tim. 3:16–17).

Third, the church is sanctified by the truth (John 17:17). The church is called to be holy and to mature in holiness, and holiness comes only by the Word of God (Eph. 5:26). The church exists, moreover, to be God's means of sanctification. That is to say, it is through the church that God's people are purified and molded into the perfect image of the Lord Jesus Christ (Eph. 4:13).

Fourth, the church is the steward of the truth. The very thing that establishes the unity and purity of the saints is the very thing the church has been entrusted with—the truth (Jude 3). As stewards, the church is called to believe, obey, defend, and proclaim the truth.

Fifth, the church is the confessor of truth. The mission of the church is to evangelize unbelievers and disciple believers with the truth of God's Word (Matt. 28:19–20). This is why Martyn Lloyd-Jones stated, "The primary task of the Church and of the Christian minister is the preaching of the Word of God."[10] The church is to come together to worship God by communicating the truth through preaching God's Word, singing God's Word, praying God's Word, and seeing God's Word in observing the ordinances. In these divinely prescribed methods, the church carries out its purpose by being what God designed it to be—the pillar and ground of truth.

---

10 Martyn Lloyd-Jones, *Preaching and Preachers* (Grand Rapids: Zondervan, 2011), 26.

And it is because of this that the Reformers and Puritans placed doctrinal preaching and observance of the ordinances as critical to the church's very existence. As Article 7 of the Augsburg Confession (1530) states, "The Church is the congregation of saints, in which the Gospel is rightly taught and the Sacraments are rightly administered." Likewise, John Calvin said, "Wherever we see the Word of God purely preached and heard, and the sacraments administered according to Christ's institution, there, it is not to be doubted, a church of God exists."[11]

The church lives by the truth. Without the truth, the church ceases to exist. In a postmodern age where the culture is shaped by relativism, subjectivity, and pragmatism, the church is the one light that shines forth the truth in the darkness.

To carry out this objective, God has given the church pastors and teachers to oversee the work of the ministry (Eph. 4:8–16). Consequently, the local church is not without any formal structure, membership, leadership, and discipline. Rather, as we shall see in chapter 5, Christ has prescribed a certain form of organization and leadership to His church. God has called local churches to be ruled by their ordained leaders (Acts 20:28). When Paul addressed the church at Philippi, for instance, he greeted not only "all the saints in Christ Jesus who are at Philippi" but their "overseers and deacons" too (Phil. 1:1). The church has the power to ordain its elders and deacons as well as the power to exercise its prescribed discipline (Matt. 18:15–20). Without the organization, leadership, and discipline prescribed to the church, a church is not in submission to its head—Jesus Christ.

___

11 Calvin, *Institutes*, 4.1.9.

Conclusion

What is the church? Simply put, the church is God's communion. But to be more precise, the three essential marks of the church need to be included in our definition. The church is God's

1. *unified communion*, which consists of all those who have been invisibly united to Christ and to each other and are visibly manifested in local assemblies that fellowship and work together for their own individual and corporate benefit.

2. *holy communion*, which consists of those who have been set apart by the Spirit and are being sanctified and molded into the perfect image of Christ Jesus.

3. *truth-bearing communion*, which, under its ordained office-bearers and discipline, preaches the Word and observes the ordinances.

In sum, if we add these three essential marks—*unity*, *purity*, and *verity*—together, the church is the communion of the saints, consisting of Christ's unified and sanctified people, who have committed themselves to upholding the truth through assembling together with their ordained leaders as they give themselves to worshiping God by preaching the Word, observing the ordinances, and exercising discipline.

Understanding the nature of the church is vital because it's the nature of the church that determines the membership, authority, purpose, and worship of the church. Since the church is holy and unified in the truth by its very nature, the church is called to be holy and unified in the truth in its participants, purposes, and practices.

Review Questions

1. What are the three marks of the church?

2. Why does the church belong to the Lord?

3. Why are cults and false religions not a church?

4. Why is a building not a church?

5. How does Christ build His church?

6. Why is the gospel the only way of growing the church?

7. How is the church united?

8. Why is the universal church invisible?

9. Why are believers united to Christ before they are united to the body of Christ?

10. Why does the invisible and universal church manifest itself in visible and local assemblies?

11. Why do Christians need one another?

12. Why is holiness one of the marks of the church?

13. How should holiness impact the membership and discipline of the church?

14. How is the church the "pillar and ground" of truth?

15. How should the marks of the church shape the purpose and mission of the church?

16. What do you think most people are looking for in a church?

17. What should believers look for when choosing a church?

2

The Membership of the Church

GOD CALLS HIS PEOPLE to be active and faithful members of a local church. Going to church is not to be squeezed into the Christian's weekly schedule; rather, it should be the principal activity and focal point of the Christian life. Entertainment, hobbies, work, and family are secondary to the worship of God in the assembly of the saints. In other words, Christians are to rotate their schedules around the life of the church.

The primary reason for going to church is not to become a better parent, spouse, worker, or citizen but, rather, to worship God. Those who only go to church to gain skills to better cope with life's problems have misunderstood the purpose of the church. Sure, church will help the Christian in all areas of life, but the ultimate goal of the Christian is not self, work, or family *but God*. Christians are to go to church to glorify God, and if God is to be the center of the Christian life (and the center of the Christian family), then church is to be the center of the Christian schedule.

An Aversion to Church Membership

Yet, sadly, this seems too extreme for many professing Christians. Even if they admit that worship is to take priority over every other activity of life, too many of them still feel that they can worship God just as well apart from other Christians (e.g., in their homes privately listening to or watching an online sermon or by going for a walk in the woods) as they can in a gathered assembly of the saints.

An Aversion to Accountability

The individuality and personal freedom of post-modernism have won over contemporary Christianity. Today's postmodern believer views the Christian life, for the most part, independently of the body of Christ. And when church attendance is factored in, a peculiar flavor of church that fits one's personality and particular set of desires must meet the match. The "young and restless" are looking for a church on the cutting edge. Senior citizens are looking for traditional worship. Parents are looking for a nursery. The youth are looking for cool activities. Single adults are looking for "love." Viewing the church through the lens of "self" leads people to judge a church based on how well the church meets their personal expectations.

Many churches have compounded the problem by catering to this type of individualism. To satisfy man's free spirit, individualism has been exalted above corporate community, and creating an atmosphere where people can enjoy their own individual "experience" has become more important for the church than upholding and promoting their doctrinal standards and confessions. "Church" has become a place for people to get a "spiritual experience" rather than being a place for mutual accountability and biblical instruction for corporate interaction. Consequently, churches no longer have a formal membership policy but simply view everyone—both believers and non-believers—as attendees. Church has become like a fast-food restaurant: drive in, get fed, and drive out, with no commitments attached.

This type of individualism, of course, is undermining church membership. With a low view of accountability, Christians have begun to believe that church membership is optional. They see it as a good thing, maybe, but not a biblical necessity. Many people are content to church hop their whole lives or stay at home. Option B is to go to the woods to worship God in their own way or to attend a church but never become committed and submitted to a church.

An Aversion to Commitment

Even when people do join a church, remaining committed and faithful is not to be expected. No longer are people leaving a church because of doctrinal error or other biblical concerns but because they hear about all the excitement that is coming from the new church down the road. Rather than remaining faithful to the body of believers with whom they have united themselves, they eagerly run down the street to join the enthusiasm. People will also jump ship if they get their feelings hurt. Postmodernists are quick to change membership for the slightest reason. Gone are the days where Christians remain faithful to a church and seek to work out their differences with love and humility. Paul's advice for Euodia and Syntyche "to agree in the Lord" (Phil. 4:2) is no longer worth it. We now hear, "You've got to find a church that is right for you."

I guess this uncommitted spirit is not all that new; even the Puritan theologian John Owen complained of church hoppers in the late seventeenth century:

> Nor do we in the least approve of their practice, who, upon every failing of these things in the church, think themselves sufficiently warranted immediately of their own minds to depart from its communion. Much more do we condemn them who suffer themselves in these things to be guided by their

own surmises and misapprehensions; for such there may be as make their own hasty conceptions to be the rule of all church administrations and communion, who, unless they are in all things pleased, can be quiet nowhere.[1]

This type of independence is distressing because it is contrary to the truth of God's Word and the unity of the brethren. Although all Christians have an individual and personal relationship with Christ, they are also called by God to live out their Christianity within the community of God's people. Christianity is personal but not individualistic. In fact, it is their personal and invisible relationship with Christ that compels believers to have a corporate and visible relationship with each other. The same Spirit who unites believers to Christ is the Spirit who unites believers to each other. To love Christ is to love His people, and to submit to Christ is to submit to a local church.

Some Christians who live great distances from a solid church may have no alternative but to listen to recorded sermons at home with other believers for a season. But Christians should never become content with this as a long-term solution.

Some professing Christians have countless excuses for taking church membership lightly. A spirit of individualism is alive and well. An aversion to commitment, submission, and accountability is also prevalent. Yet, regardless of the excuse, the Christian life is not designed to be experienced independent of faithful and active membership within a community of a biblically organized assembly of the saints—the local church.

Reasons to Join a Church

If the church is God's united and sanctified people who have been entrusted with the truth (see chapter 1), then it only makes sense

---

1 John Owen, "Discourse on Christian Love and Peace," in *The Works of John Owen* (Edinburgh: Banner of Truth, 1998), 15:96.

that God's people assemble in local congregations. The Bible does not view church membership as optional for the believer. Though you may not think active church membership is all that important, there are at least six reasons why being accountable to a local church is a necessity.

1. Church Membership Is Assumed in the New Testament

Some people view the local church as a social club or a type of volunteer association. The church, however, is not a volunteer society that people are free to join and leave at their own pleasure. Those who think this way may argue that the Bible does not require Christians to formally unite to a local church. Yet the New Testament assumes that Christians are members of a local church. Like baptism, church membership does not save sinners, but also like baptism, church membership is not viewed as a choice.

The New Testament does not define the church as a volunteer society. Instead, the church is viewed in Scripture as a family. A family is not something anyone chooses but is something one is united to by birth—and for the church, by the *new birth*. For this reason, Michael Horton rightly claims: "A church is not a group of friends you've picked; it's a group of brothers and sisters God has picked for you."[2] Though we may have to choose (because of the plurality of congregations) which assembly to join, choosing to forsake the church altogether is not a biblical option.

Moreover, the organic and natural process of salvation is (1) faith, (2) baptism, and (3) church membership. For, as Luke recorded in the book of Acts, "Those who received his word were baptized, and there were added [to the church] that day about three thousand souls. And they devoted themselves to the apostles'

2   Michael Horton (@MichaelHorton_), Twitter, December 30, 2016, https://twitter.com/michaelhorton_/status/814737287951040512.

teaching and the fellowship, by breaking of bread and the prayers" (Acts 2:41–42). In a way of explanation, Jonathan Leeman says:

> From the non-Christian's standpoint, a local church is a voluntary association. No one has to join. From the standpoint of the Christian, however, it's not. Once you choose Christ, you must choose his people, too. It's a package deal. Choose the Father and the Son and you have to choose the whole family— which you do through a local church.[3]

Furthermore, the New Testament was written under the assumption that Christians are members of local churches because it was primarily written not to disconnected individuals but to various local churches. How did Paul communicate to the individual saints? He communicated to them by addressing his letters to churches and by having his letters read aloud in their gathered assemblies (Col. 4:16).

With the assumption that believers are members of a local church, Paul wrote his epistles, such as 1 Timothy, so that they "may know how one ought to behave in the household of God, which is the church of the living God" (1 Tim. 3:14–15). If we need to know how to behave ourselves in the church, it implies that we are a member of a church. In fact, much of the responsibilities of the Christian life cannot be carried out independently of church membership. James Bannerman understood this when he stated:

> Alone with God, I must realize the Bible as if it were a message from Him to my solitary self, singled out and separated from other men, and feeling my own individual responsibility in receiving or rejecting it. But the Bible does not stop here: it deals with man, not only as a solitary unit in his relation to God, but also as a member of a spiritual society, gathered together in the name of Jesus. It is not a mere system of doctrines to be believed and precepts to be observed by each individual Christian independently of others, and apart from others: it is

---

3 Jonathan Leeman, *Church Membership* (Wheaton, IL: Crossway, 2012), 31.

a system of doctrines and precepts, designed and adapted for a society of Christians.[4]

In other words, much of the New Testament cannot be properly understood and fully applied without the existence of church membership.

In addition, the apostle Paul was not content in seeing individual conversions. Paul was more than an evangelist; he was a church planter. He would either labor long enough in a particular location to establish a local church, or he would send a coworker, such as Silas or Timothy, to those regions until a self-governing church was raised up. Planting churches was important for Paul because the maturity of the saints was important to him. And if the apostle Paul spent so much energy planting and establishing churches, why would any Christian think they are exempt from needing to be an active member of a church?

So, for these three reasons—the church is a family, the New Testament was written to churches, and Paul was a church planter— the New Testament assumes that Christians are members of a local church. And if this is the assumption of the Scriptures, then it must be granted that church membership is a biblical requirement for believers.

2. Church Membership Is Evidence of the New Birth

If the natural order is faith, baptism, then church membership (Acts 2:41, 47), then church membership is evidence of the new birth. For this reason, Mark Dever says: "When a person becomes a Christian, he doesn't just join a local church because it's a good habit for growing in spiritual maturity. He joins a local church because it's the expression of what Christ has *made him*—a member of the body

---

4 James Bannerman, *The Church of Christ* (Edinburgh: Banner of Truth, 1974), 1:2.

of Christ."[5] Jay Adams went as far as to say: "Church membership was so important that Paul and Silas baptized the Philippian jailer into the membership of Christ's church at midnight with Paul's back still bloody from a beating! He did not even wait till morning! Identification with Christ's church is important; without it, one must be treated 'as a heathen and publican.'"[6]

Because of their spiritual union in the body of Christ, Christians are drawn together by an internal force. For this reason, James Bannerman claimed:

> Were there no positive command or appointment requiring Christians to unite together and to form on earth a society joined together by the profession of the same faith, the very nature of Christianity would force such a result. In the profession of it in common, men would find themselves insensibly drawn to other believers with a power not to be resisted; and in the bounds of the same Savior and the same Spirit they would feel and own a nearer tie than that of kindred, and a holier relationship than one of blood. In common joy and sorrows which Christians and none but Christians share, in the one faith and one Savior in which they rejoice together in same hopes and fears, the same sin escaped, and the same Salvation won, in which they participate, there is a union of the most intimate kind produced and cemented, which is not with them a matter of choice, but a matter of inevitable necessity.[7]

The saints love one another, they care for one another, and they feel closest to heaven when they are together. In the past, and in certain countries, persecution, distress, and various threats could not deter Christians from regularly assembling. Christians of old often met in the forests, fields, or even in dark dens or caves. They

5 Mark Dever, *What Is a Healthy Church?* (Wheaton, IL: Crossway, 2007), 26, emphasis original.
6 Jay Adams, *Handbook of Church Discipline* (Grand Rapids: Zondervan, 1986), 81n3.
7 Bannerman, *Church of Christ*, 1:19.

did not mind traveling many miles in difficult conditions. All they knew was that they loved the Lord and desired to meet with the brethren to worship the living God collectively and enjoy the fellowship of the saints. If someone does not love the brethren, even in their imperfect and unglorified state, then one must wonder if that person is truly born again into the family of God (1 John 3:14).

3. Church Membership Is Essential for Sanctification

The reason church membership is evidence of the new birth is that the Scripture teaches that when believers are united to Christ by the new birth, they are also *mutually* united into one body. This union is not merely symbolic or hypothetical but is purposeful in the productivity and functioning of every Christian. Christians are interwoven in such a fashion that they cannot properly function apart from one another (1 Cor. 12). Therefore, the notion that a Christian can operate and please God apart from the rest of the body of Christ is not only a prideful misconception, it's an impossibility.

4. Church Membership Is Essential to Loving Christ

Christ loves the church enough to die for the church (Eph. 5:25). And though the church is not yet perfected (Eph. 5:26–27), Christ still loves the church. Therefore, how are we going to love Christ without loving that which He also loves? How can we say we love the Head of the church if we don't also say we love the body of Christ—even in its imperfect state? To tell your spouse that you only love their head and not their body is an insult that will not go over very well. In the same way, by loving Christ, we are called to love the church. For this reason, I agree with Joel Beeke who asked: "If the Lord Jesus Christ cherished the Church so much that He died for her, is it too much for Him to ask His followers to cherish the Church and live for her?"[8]

---

8 Joel Beeke, "Glorious Things of Thee Are Spoken" in *Onward Christian Soldiers*, ed. Don Kistler (Morgan, PA: Soli Deo Gloria, 1999), 33.

5. Church Membership Is Essential to Obedience

The Bible makes it clear that we are to be active members of a local church when it says, "And let us consider how to stir up one another to love and good works, not neglecting to meet together, as is the habit of some, but encouraging one another, and all the more as you see the Day drawing near" (Heb. 10:24–25). With this command in mind, Charles Spurgeon addressed the necessity of church membership for those who falsely think they do not need to submit to a local church body:

> I know there are some who say, "Well, I've given myself to the Lord, but I don't intend to give myself to any church." I say, "Now why not?" And they answer, "Because I can be just as good a Christian without it." I say, "Are you quite clear about that? You can be as good a Christian by disobedience to your Lord's commands as by being obedient? I don't believe that you're answering the purpose for which Christ saved you. You're living contrary to the life which Christ would have you live and you are much to blame for the injury you do."[9]

Not only is church membership a direct command but many other commands in Scripture cannot be obeyed without being an active member of a local church:

- ❧ One could not obey ruling elders (Heb. 13:17).

- ❧ One could not properly participate in the Lord's Supper (1 Cor. 10:17).

- ❧ One could not come together with other Christians for corporate worship (Col. 3:16).

Therefore, according to Charles Hodge: "The independency of one Christian of all others . . . is inconsistent with the relation in

---

9   Quoted in Tom Carter, *Charles Spurgeon at His Best* (Grand Rapids: Baker, 1988), 34.

which believers stand to each other, and with the express commands of Scripture."[10]

6. Church Membership Is God's Means of Accountability

Church membership is more than getting our names on the church role and our phone numbers and pictures in the church directory. It is more than just the outward acknowledgment that we will make a particular church our new church home. Serious commitments and sobering consequences are involved in church membership. At the heart of church membership is accountability. We are called to commit and to submit to one another. The church is designed to minister, love, care, and watch over its members. This means that each member has a responsibility to love and pray for the body of Christ.

Conclusion

If we jump from church to church and move our membership from here to there so casually, it reveals that we don't deem church membership as all that important. What is behind this take-it-or-leave-it mentality? It is the perspective that the church is to be handled in the same way as the favorite local movie theater. Church has become nothing more than a spectator sport, another place of entertainment to go on Sunday with no strings attached.

The fact that Christ died for the church must elevate it as more than just a Sunday morning punch-in, punch-out activity for us. Church membership is something that God requires of His people, which includes placing oneself under the care of the church and under the rule of the elders, committing to be faithful in attendance and a regular supporter of the ministry, and making oneself responsible for the spiritual well-being of others within the

---

10 Charles Hodge, *Commentary on the Epistle to the Ephesians* (Grand Rapids: Eerdmans, 1994), 31.

church body. Christ instituted the church for the saints; to shun it is to view oneself wiser than God (Matt. 16:18).

Other reasons could be given for church membership, but these are more than enough to prove that God requires His people to live out their Christian lives in the context of being active and faithful to a local body of believers. Much more needs to be said about the blessings and responsibility of church members, how local assemblies are to be established and governed, and what functions they are to carry out in their organized meetings, but at this point in our study, it is clear that church membership is not optional for the followers of Christ.

Review Questions

1. Is being committed and submitted to a local church optional? Why or why not?

2. Why should the worship and functions of the local church take priority in our weekly schedules?

3. What are some unbiblical reasons people have for not remaining faithful to a local church?

4. Why is submission to a church so important?

5. Why is accountability so important?

6. Is there any acceptable reason for not joining a local church? Explain.

7. List at least three reasons why believers should be committed and submitted to a local church?

8. Why is church membership so important for Christians?

9. What are justifiable reasons for leaving a local church?

10. How should we leave a church?

11. Why does God require church membership?

3

The Duties of
Church Membership

EVERY CHRISTIAN HAS BOTH the responsibility and privilege of partaking and sharing in the spiritual giftedness that God has given the church. Every Christian has been engrafted into the body of Christ and personally gifted by the Holy Spirit (Rom. 12:6) to assist the spiritual growth of the greater body of Christ (Eph. 4:16). Because the church, as the communion of the saints, is God's official truth bearer, consisting of those who have been sanctified and united together in Christ Jesus, and who regularly assemble to worship God through observing the ordinances and listening to the preached Word, the principal duties and privileges of every church member are to maintain *unity* through maturing in personal and corporate *holiness* by growing in the knowledge of the *truth*. In other words, the priority of every church member includes three basic things: *unity*, *purity*, and *verity*.

Unity

Christian unity is a beautiful thing in the eyes of God. It is more than the absence of discord, as it includes warm fellowship saturated with love and goodwill. "Behold," David says, "how good and pleasant it is when brothers dwell in unity" (Ps. 133:1). There is nothing like collectively worshiping God with a unified heart and mind—it is the closest thing to heaven on earth.

This unity is established by the common fellowship Christians have in Christ Jesus. The church is one body united by one Spirit (Eph. 4:5). This unity is deeper than a shared interest, for it is rooted in the spiritual life that all God's people share in Christ Jesus.

Therefore, "Christians are not exhorted to create a unity among themselves," Alan Stibbs stated, "as though none existed. Rather they are told to give diligence first to preserve, and then to give full and mature expression to, the Spirit-given unity which God has created. Such unity, by its very nature, is fostered and consummated as fellow-believers in Christ enjoy and express together their fellowship with the one Lord in the one Spirit."[1]

But, sadly, not all churches experience such unity. Fractions, discord, and cliques can abound in churches. This is because of two things. One, as wheat and tares often grow together, unbelievers are mixed within the member-ship of the church. Without spiritual regeneration, there is no unity in the Spirit. Two, though Christians have a new nature and are united to Christ and to each other, they still struggle with sin. Christians can be prideful, harsh, and hurtful. Wherever unforgiveness and pride reside, unity will have a difficult time thriving. Therefore, because no perfect church exists, every church member is called to fight sin and labor to maintain "the unity of the Spirit in the bond of peace" (Eph. 4:3).

Members Are to Be Active and Faithful in Attendance

Maintaining the unity that God has established begins with active and faithful church membership, for Christ did not design the Christian life to be lived out in isolation and in separation from

---

1 Alan Stibbs, *God's People* (London: IVF, 1959), 46.

the other members of His spiritual body. Spiritual life and gifts are designed by God to function within the context of the local church. By being united to Christ, we become united to the other members of the body of Christ (Rom. 12:5). This means that our own spiritual growth and maturity is interconnected with the spiritual growth and maturity of the body of Christ. According to Alan Stibbs, "Different members complement one another. They are meant to realize and to enjoy life in Christ together, and in the service of one another." For this reason, Stibbs went on to state:

> As Christians we can be kept fully fit and grow to maturity, and fulfill our divinely-intended service, only by active co-operation with our fellow Christians. Every member of Christ's body the Church has his proper and necessary contribution to make to the well-being of the whole. None can be despised or disregarded without damage and loss to the body corporate.[2]

And if we need the church to function and mature properly, then we need to be active and faithful to the functions and life of the church. "An inactive church member," according to Joel Beeke, "is a contradiction in terms. If we do not cherish the Church and view membership as a great privilege, we need to question if we are truly a part of the Church."[3]

Christians are commanded to maintain fellowship with the saints (1 John 1:7) and not to forsake the local assembling of themselves together (Heb. 10:25). Therefore, when Christians leave a church to worship at home, they are failing to maintain the unity of the Spirit.

Members Are to Serve Each Other

Not only do we need the spiritual gifts of other Christians, but other Christians also need our spiritual gifts. And if others need

---

2   Stibbs, *God's People*, 46.

3   Joel Beeke, "Glorious Things of Thee Are Spoken" in *Onward Christian Soldiers*, ed. Don Kistler (Morgan, PA: Soli Deo Gloria, 1999), 39.

what God has given us, then we are responsible to help them (Rom. 12:3–8). "Every Christian," the renowned Princeton theologian Charles Hodge claimed, "is responsible for his faith and conduct to his brother in the Lord, because he constitutes with them one body having a common faith and a common life."[4] In other words, God has not called or gifted us to be self-focused. Rather, God has called us to use our gifts and resources to assist the growth of His body. It is our responsibility, as Don Whitney explains, to serve the church:

> When God makes body parts, whether for physical bodies or spiritual bodies, He makes them for a specific function in a specific body. Regardless of your educational level, IQ, experience, or talents, if you are a Christian you have a Christ-intended function in the church. You are there for a reason. You aren't there just for yourself and what you can get out of the church. God's plan for the church involves every member ministering to the rest of the church. For in this way each of us supplies something of Christ to others.[5]

Hence, we have a duty to live for the Lord not only for our own spiritual profit but also for the profit of our brothers and sisters in Christ. It is not a coincidence, then, that the members of the body of Christ have been gifted unequally and differently. And these different spiritual gifts should not be wasted on independent self-consumption. For Christians to refrain from the fellowship of saints and to remain inactive in the body of Christ is to misuse the measure of grace that has been deposited in them by God. Therefore, each member of the body is to carry out their function and exercise their spiritual gifts for the overall benefit of the body (Rom. 12:3–8). As the apostle Paul says, "Let each of you look not only to his own interests, but also to the interests of others" (Phil. 2:4).

4 Charles Hodge, *Commentary on the Epistle to the Ephesians* (Grand Rapids: Eerdmans, 1994), 310.

5 Donald S. Whitney, "To Her My Toils and Cares Be Giv'n" in *Onward Christian Soldiers*, ed. Don Kistler (Morgan, PA: Soli Deo Gloria, 1999), 196–97.

The benefit for each member of the body of Christ is enormous. All the foot needs to do is help the body to walk, and in return, the foot has the eyes to help him see, the hand to help him work, and the rest of the body, attached to its life-giving Head—Jesus Christ—to assist him in becoming a complete man, lacking nothing. Since these gifts of God are designed for the edification of the body of Christ, then the local church, the only visible and tangible reality of that body, is the proper setting for Christians to exercise their gifts (Rom. 12; 1 Cor. 12). Thus, every church member is called by God to love (1 Peter 1:22), care (1 Cor. 12:24–26), pray (James 5:16), honor (Rom. 12:10), and submit (Eph. 5:21) to one another as unto the Lord.

Members Are to Love and Honor Each Other

Strife and discord are easy to sow in the church. But woe to those who plant such wicked seeds in God's vineyard. God hates sin, and it is a sin—a great sin—to sow "discord among [the] brethren" (Prov. 6:19 KJV). That which divides God's people and tears the unity of the church is a great sin indeed. If we are commanded to maintain unity, we must realize that we sin against God when we initiate dissension among the saints.

Paul, therefore, exhorts us "to walk in a manner worthy of the calling to which you have been called, with all humility and gentleness, with patience, bearing with one another in love, eager to maintain the unity of the Spirit in the bond of peace" (Eph. 4:1–3). Listed here are many of the traits needed for unity: humility, gentleness, patience, and love. The command is for us to utilize these traits to "maintain the unity of the Spirit." This exhortation implies that unity cannot be taken for granted. Selfishness still exists within us all, and sin will continue to occur within the church. This is why patience, forgiveness, and love are necessary attributes for the saints. If there were no selfishness and hypocrisy in the church, there would be no need for long-suffering and forgiveness. Yet, long-suffering and forgiveness are required because the danger of discord and factions are ever present. We are all called to exhibit and display the fruit of the Spirit because we have been charged by God to do all we can to maintain the unity that has been established by the Spirit. If we disregard this charge, we are living in sin.

With this in mind, we must guard our hearts. Before discord erupts openly, it usually takes place inwardly. Once we become critical and unhappy with a few things—without properly dealing with our concerns—we will begin looking for problems. And once we start looking for problems, the floodgates will open, and we'll see offenses everywhere. Though we may not leave the church immediately, our affections have already started to pull away from the congregation. Though we still attend bodily, our hearts have already exited. Slowly but increasingly, we will start missing church functions, until we remove ourselves altogether—causing a breach in the unity of the church.

We must remember that it is a sin to harbor animosity for a fellow church member without seeking reconciliation (Prov. 10:18). To be secretly offended without seeking to forgive will separate friendships and fracture the unity of the church. Thus, we must be careful to guard our hearts against all forms of resentment, envy, and pride. We must maintain a love for our brothers and never allow bitterness or contention to separate our affections from the people of God.

A critical spirit is contagious. It can spread quickly throughout the congregation. Subtle complaints, even when legitimate, often breed discontentment, and discontentment often spreads until it causes division within the church. Though there may be proper concerns, these complaints can be mishandled and cause discord.

It often starts with a simple concern, but the concern soon turns into gossip. Rather than seeking to handle the problem biblically, the problem is often communicated to others. Moreover, it is natural for us when we hear criticism to respond with our own criticism.

We become critical, and our critical spirits influence others to be critical. Not only have we sinned in our own hearts, but we have also led others into this sin. We have ceased to promote unity, but instead have sown seeds of discord among the saints.

It is not wrong to have concerns, but once we take pleasure in pointing out flaws and sharing these flaws with others, we have failed to operate in love. We have spoken against our brothers, and this is a transgression against God's law (James 4:11). Minor concerns should be overlooked—for love covers such things (1 Peter 4:8). When concerns need to be addressed, they should be directed only to the people directly involved. This should be done in the spirit of humility and with the desire to resolve the issue and the goal of strengthening the unity of the Spirit (Gal. 6:1).

Leaving the church out the back door without seeking to resolve one's differences is also not a good solution. Though some may think they are seeking to not disrupt the unity of the church by leaving quietly, they are still leaving with unresolved differences without any opportunity for a biblical resolution. If it is disrespectful to leave a friendship without expiation, it is even more disrespectful to leave a church without first seeking to resolve the differences that may exist. Sadly, too many are too quick to leave a church.

A way to maintain unity when we hear others complain about the church is to redirect that criticism with words of grace. Paul commands us that we are to "let no corrupting talk come out of [our] mouths, but only such as is good for building up, as fits the occasion, that it may give grace to those who hear" (Eph. 4:29). This command is to be implemented in every situation. If our communication is not seeking to assist others in their walk with the Lord, then we must refrain from speaking until the Spirit and His Word re-tunes our hearts.

So, when a fellow church member begins whispering in our ear, there is no need to tell that person that they are in danger of gossiping. We need only to redirect the conversation. One of the best ways to redirect gossip is by saying, "You are concerned about John Doe? We love John Doe. Have you addressed your concern with him? If not, I will be happy to go with you." This usually does the trick. Regardless, the goal is to always respond in a way that seeks to reconcile and build up our precious brothers and sisters—not to tear them down. If we, however, enter into their gossip, we share in their guilt. It is our duty not only to seek to defend the honor of our brothers and sisters but to assist others in refraining from slander.

For this reason, we are commanded to be "of the same mind, having the same love, being in full accord and of one mind [by doing] nothing from selfish ambition or conceit, but in humility count[ing] others more significant than [ourselves]" (Phil. 2:2–3). In short, we are to "love one another with brotherly affection, [and] outdo one another in showing honor" (Rom. 12:10).

Purity

Although faith is the only requirement to join the universal body of Christ, something more should be needed to join a local church—visible holiness. Once the invisible church becomes manifested in a local and visible society, then some outward form of affirmation is needed to recognize who belongs to its fellowship. That is, faith must be tangibly demonstrated to join a local church. Because the local church cannot see the heart, it must judge one's profession by their works of faith. John Owen identified the requirement for local church membership as "a double profession, one by *words*, the other by *works*."[6] In other words, a person needs not only a profession of faith but a life that is in agreement with that profession (Matt. 3:8).

Practically speaking, local churches are responsible for reserving church membership only for those who maintain their Christian testimony. Joel Beeke says, "It is a scandal when churches

6 John Owen, "The Nature of the Gospel Church," in *The Works of John Owen* (Edinburgh: Banner of Truth, 1995), 16:18.

list dozens, sometimes hundreds, of families on their rolls of membership who seldom attend worship services and show that they have no personal faith in Christ, no living relationship with Him."[7]

Members Are to Live Holy Lives

It follows that church membership is exclusively for believers whose lives are in agreement with their testimony. As the book of James plainly teaches, the only way for the church to see this inward faith is by observing a changed life—a life that is characterized by obedience to God and a love for the brethren.

Members Are to Promote Holiness in Others

Personal holiness is not only beneficial for the individual, but also for the body of Christ. Church members who are zealously living for the Lord throughout the week will be of a greater benefit to the church on Sunday than those who are plagued with worldliness. Thus, we must keep in mind that we have a responsibility to live a holy life, not just for ourselves but for others. If we are called to promote holiness in others, it starts with living a holy life. This duty also includes our words. We are called to encourage, rebuke, and pray for others in our common pursuit of holiness. For the Lord has called us to "consider how to stir up one another to love and good works" (Heb. 10:24).

Members Are to Partake of the Church Ordinances

One reason why believers should be baptized is that it demonstrates to the church their willingness to be submissive to God (Acts 2:38). And the Lord's Supper is reserved for only believers who are in good standing with the body of Christ (1 Cor. 11:24). Without faith toward God and a clean conscience toward man, members

---

7 Beeke, "Glorious Things," 39.

should refrain from partaking Communion, which speaks of our communion and fellowship with Christ and His body.

Members Are to Carry Out Church Discipline

The Scriptures also teach that church members are required to carry out discipline for fellow members who fall into habitual or unrepentant sin (2 Thess. 3:14–15). If a church member is living in sin and refuses to heed the admonishment of the church, the church is required (by the authority of Christ) to discipline the unrepentant member in hopes of restoration (Gal. 6:1).

Verity

Sound doctrine is not just the concern of the elders, it is the responsibility of every member of the church. The individual members of the church are called to grow in unity and purity through growing in the knowledge of the truth (Eph. 4:13–16). Thus, we are all called to embrace, confess, guard, and support the truth as those who have been redeemed and transformed by the truth.

Members Are to Confess the Truth

Every member is required to believe and confess the truth of the gospel. This is nonnegotiable. The gospel of Jesus Christ consists of the essential truths that must be believed for one to be counted and treated as a Christian.

The gospel includes the soul-saving doctrines that must be embraced to be a Christian, such as the deity and humanity and sinlessness and death and resurrection and ascension and return of Jesus Christ. Some truths cannot be rejected or disbelieved without the severest consequences. This is why each person must profess faith in the historical Christ of the Bible if they are to be permitted into the membership of the church.

Members Are to Be Students of the Truth

Every church member is called to be a lover and a student of the truth. Doctrine is for every believer. This is because every believer lives by faith (Rom. 1:17), and "faith comes from hearing, and hearing through the word of Christ" (Rom. 10:17). Believers are not only justified by faith (Rom. 5:1), they are sanctified by faith (Acts 26:18). Without faith it is impossible to please God (Heb. 11:6). And for our faith to grow, our knowledge of the truth must grow. Therefore, every church member is called to be a student of the Word.

Members Are to Be Transmitters of the Truth

In addition to studying God's Word, we are called to transmit His Word. This not only includes evangelizing the lost but also fellowshipping with the saints. Spiritual conversation among the saints is vital for the spiritual health of the church. As iron sharpens iron, the saints sharpen each other by exhorting and encouraging one another in the truth (Prov. 27:17). We are to address "one another in psalms and hymns and spiritual songs" (Eph. 5:19), and we are to comfort (1 Thess. 4:18), exhort (Heb. 3:13), admonish (Rom. 15:14), and edify one another (1 Thess. 5:11). Much of the work of the ministry comes by the individual members speaking to and caring for one another.

Members Are to Financially Support the Truth

The pulpit ministry is every member's responsibility. We are either called to preach to others or called to financially support those who preach to us. God has appointed pastors, who give themselves to preaching, to be financially supported by the church. Though some pastors, out of necessity, are bi-vocational, ideally they should be fully supported by the church so they can commit themselves to prayer and administering the Word (Acts 6:4). And if pastors are to give their lives to prayer and sermon preparation and delivery, it is the church's responsibility to support them (Gal. 6:6), for "the Lord commanded that those who proclaim the gospel should get their living by the gospel" (1 Cor. 9:14).

Not only is this a financial responsibility of the church, it is the *chief* financial responsibility of the church. Though churches may have other expenses, such as building outlays and operating costs, the only expense the Scriptures mandate for the church is the support of its ministers.

This makes it every member's responsibility to support the work of the ministry. Though it is a blessing to aid the poor or to give to our favorite parachurch ministry or to support a missionary directly, our main obligation is to support the ministry of our own local church. For the apostle Paul says, "If we have sown spiritual things among you, is it too much if we reap material things from you?" (1 Cor. 9:11). In other words, it is our duty to give physically to those who are giving to us spiritually.

Conclusion

It goes without saying that church membership is to be taken seriously. The church is not a movie theater where we can enter in and out at our own pleasure without any commitments. Unlike the theater, the church is a sacred place of accountability and responsibilities.

We could look at all these responsibilities as a burden, but that would be unhelpful and a misconception. Rather, we should view these responsibilities as privileges. To love and serve the visible body of Christ on earth is to love and serve the invisible Christ in heaven. This includes benefiting others and being benefited by others.

What a joy and privilege it is to be a member of Christ's church. This is why Martyn Lloyd-Jones said: "We must re-grasp the idea of church membership as being the membership of the body of Christ and as the biggest honour which can come man's way in this world."[8]

---

8   Martyn Lloyd-Jones, *Knowing the Times* (Edinburgh: Banner of Truth, 1989), 30.

Review Questions

1. Why is church membership more than just church attendance?

2. Do Christians have responsibilities toward their local church?

3. Where should our spiritual gifts be principally used?

4. What does it mean to strive to maintain the unity of the Spirit?

5. Why are humility and love so important in maintaining church unity?

6. Why is personal holiness a responsibility to the church?

7. How does our lack of holiness impact the holiness of our local churches?

8. How are we, as individuals, to uphold the truth within our local churches?

9. Why is financially supporting your own local church a biblical mandate?

Part 2

The Authority of the Church

Truly, I say to you, whatever you bind on earth shall be bound in heaven, and whatever you loose on earth shall be loosed in heaven.

Matthew 18:18

4

The Power and Discipline
of the Church

GOD HAS GRANTED THE CHURCH power and authority. The church is not a weak configuration of people gathering together by their own initiative and making up their own objectives and regulations as they go. The church is not a man-made social club that creates its own rules of administration. Rather, the church is a divine and holy institution equipped by God and borne along by His Spirit. The local church is a living organism that has been given authority and power by God to execute and carry out its prescribed purposes and exercise its discipline when needed.

Though the church does not have the power to write and prescribe new doctrines, laws, and ordinances (as that power belongs to Christ alone), it does have the power to publish and execute the doctrines, laws, and ordinances of Christ to make sure the members of Christ are walking in faith and obedience.

The Power of the Church

God has *not* given the church the authority to do what it wants. The church does *not* have permission to create its own objectives, to carry out its own desires, and function by its own self-made rules. The church has *no right* to bind the conscience of its membership to manufactured rules and objectives. The legislative power belongs to the head of the church, Christ Jesus, alone.

Without Christ, the Church Has No Authority

If the church abandons the Great Commission (Matt. 28:16–20) to refocus its energy and resources on social issues, the church will no longer operate under the authority and power of God. Consequently, when churches are more interested in pleasing man than pleasing God, they will no longer function with the authority of God.

And when churches operate outside of the authority of God, they will cease to operate with the power of God. Though their doors may remain open and their pews may remain full, their spiritual power and effectiveness will be depleted. Regeneration and sanctification, which are the result of the Spirit working through the supernatural power of the Word, will be replaced with false professions and carnal Christianity, the result of man using fleshly gimmicks and man-made techniques. Powerful preaching will be exchanged for lifeless motivational speeches, and the effectual prayer meetings will be substituted with a few disingenuous and ineffective petitions. There may remain a form of godliness, but the power and presence of the Spirit will be missing in churches that do not submit to God's Word.

This happens when churches fail to preach and teach the whole counsel of God. When the focus of the church becomes "churching" the unchurched, it does not take long before it becomes bankrupt of its power. How does this happen? The church abrogates its authority by putting the potential visitor in charge. When the purpose of the church becomes driven by the demands of the consumer, then the consumer holds the keys to the church. What the church perceives people want, the church seeks to supply. With churches replacing the Bible with the results of surveys, no wonder the consumer thinks so little of church authority—the consumer knows who is really in charge.

Numerical growth may deceive these churches into thinking God is still blessing their endeavors, but the ever-increasing worldliness in their membership and entertainment in their services reveals that they are merely powerless religious clubs masquerading as churches of the living God. Though churches may grow faster using wood, hay, and straw, such church-growth techniques will not build a church that will endure the fires of God's judgment (1 Cor. 3:13).

With Christ, the Church Has Authority

Though the church has no authority and power in itself, the church has divine authority and power when it is submissive to God's Word. By what authority can the church hope to carry out its weighty purposes, ordinances, and discipline? By no less than the authority of the written Word of God is its answer. Christ is the head and divine ruler of the church, and His Word is its only rule and authority. If one wonders who gave the church authority to carry out its activities, the answer is simple but profound—God Himself.

It is Christ who tells the saints to not forsake the local assembly. It is Christ who tells these local assemblies how to organize and structure themselves. It is God who tells these organized assemblies they need a plurality of leaders. It is Christ who tells them what they are to do when they gather together. It is Christ who calls the church to be submissive to each other. It is Christ who tells these assemblies to practice church discipline. In short, it is Christ who rules and governs His church.

If a local church, therefore, wants to operate with the authority and power of God, it must function under the authority of Scripture. It must obey God. It must hold its members to compliance with the

Word of God. This is because churches only have authority when they submit themselves to the Authority. In other words, the church must be under authority to have authority. Consequently, churches must refrain from being blown about by the ever-changing winds of culture and take a firm stand on the rock of God's abiding and unchanging Word. They must seek to carry out God's business in God's way if they desire to have God's power.

Therefore, when a church does what God tells it to do, it operates with divine authority and power. And with such authority and power, the gates of hell shall not prevail against it (Matt. 16:18). Its preaching will be authoritative, its prayer meetings will be effectual, and its discipline will be binding because all these activities are sanctioned and empowered by God Himself. In short, where we find true churches, we find God.

Christians are obligated to be in submission to a local church that is in submission to God. Children are called to obey their parents (Eph. 6:1), wives are called to be in submission to their husbands (Eph. 5:22), and Christians are called to be accountable to their elders (Heb. 13:17). To be out of step with God's church is to be out of step with God. To disregard its membership, to neglect its worship services, to spurn its discipline, and to reject its authority is to be a disobedient follower of God. As long as the church body functions and abides by the truth of God's Word and as long as its elders and rulers do not overstep the boundaries of the Scriptures, then the doctrine, activities, actions, and discipline of the church carry the divine approval and authority of heaven.

The Discipline of the Church

Moreover, the church's power can be seen vividly in its authority to exercise its discipline. For where there is no authority to discipline disobedience, there is no authority to command obedience. For instance, you and your spouse— not strangers—have the jurisdiction to discipline your children because only you and your spouse have the authority to tell your children how to behave. Likewise, Christ has given the church jurisdiction over its members because Christ has given the church the power to hold its members accountable to God's Word and to discipline its disobedient members.

With this said, sin is never to be treated lightly. Christians are to pursue holiness with all their heart and do all they can to crucify the lust of the flesh (Rom. 13:14). Just as individual Christians are not to tolerate besetting sins in their lives, the church is not to excuse habitual and unrepentant sin within its membership. The church must deal with the leaven before it contaminates the spiritual integrity of the whole church (1 Cor. 5:7–8). Therefore, when needed, the church is authorized and obligated by God to carry out its discipline.

The Nature and Steps of Church Discipline

Exactly what is church discipline? It is best explained in Matthew 18:15–20 and 1 Corinthians 5. In these passages, we learn that church discipline is a five-step process:

1. The Lord Jesus instructed Christians to lovingly and humbly confront other believers who have openly sinned or who have forsaken the fundamentals of the faith. This is the first step. If the person repents, the problem has been resolved, and the unity of the church can continue. No one needs to know about the sin(s) except the individuals involved. Without formally labeling it as such, Christian spouses, in effect, practice this first step of discipline within marriage.

2. In the next step of church discipline, if the sinning person does not repent, they are to be approached again, this time in the presence of a few Christians who are known to be spiritual (Matt. 18:16; Gal. 6:1).

3. If this second admonition does not prevail in bringing repentance, the third step of church discipline needs to be

exercised. The failed attempts at confrontation concerning the sin(s) that was committed (or is being committed) need to be publicly made known to the whole church body (Matt. 18:17; 1 Tim. 5:20).

4.   Again, if this public disgrace does not bring correction after ample time has been given for repentance, the church is required by God to carry out the fourth step—discharge the person from the membership of the church (Matt. 18:17; 1 Cor. 5:5–13; 2 Thess. 3:6, 14–15).

5.   The fifth step is perhaps the most difficult and, yet, the most redemptive. After a sinning member has been excommunicated, God calls every church member to remove, as much as possible, all association and fellowship with this unrepentant person (1 Cor. 5:9–13). This would even include interaction on social media. This is the actual sting of church discipline—facing life and the temptations of this world without the aid, help, benefit, and blessing of God's precious people. All true believers who face this discipline will find this to be the most effective in bringing forth correction and repentance. At any point of contact, church members should regard the offender as an unbeliever and seek to evangelize them.

The Attitude of Church Discipline

- ✺ *Spiritual* – When confronting others, we need to make sure we are spiritually qualified to correct those who have stumbled (Gal. 6:1a).

- ✺ *Gentle* – When confronting others, we need to make sure we do so in the spirit of gentleness (Gal. 6:1b).

- ✺ *Cautious* – When confronting others, we need to make sure we are not self-confident. Rather, we should be guarded against falling into the very sin we are seeking to correct (Gal. 6:1c).

The Purpose of Church Discipline

Church discipline has a threefold purpose: (1) it is a means of keeping the membership of the church pure (1 Cor. 5:6–11); (2) it is a means of restoring the wayward church member (2 Cor. 2:6–8; Gal. 6:1), and (3) it is a means of deterring others from falling into sin themselves (1 Tim. 5:20).

The Authority of Church Discipline

It is a fearful thing to be disciplined by the church. Church discipline is not a man-made invention but a loving intervention established by Christ Himself. When a church carries out discipline, it does so by the authority of heaven itself (Matt. 18:18–19). Therefore, church discipline is effective and authoritative.

The Efficacy of Church Discipline

In the day in which we live, where Christians often jump from church to church over preferences or hurt feelings, it may appear that church discipline is ineffective. But even if the results are not immediately seen, church discipline will always have a purifying effect for the local church body when carried out properly.

Because God's people are spiritually united into one body, they love one another and cannot live apart from each other. Because the local church is called to function as a community that consists of the brethren engaging in regular fellowship and mutual assistance, when a disobedient Christian is placed outside this loving fellowship, he or she feels severely deprived. To restrict a Christian from the fellowship of the brethren is like taking away an infant child from a loving mother.

This is why church discipline works. God's children find that they cannot live and be contented or joyful outside of the fellowship of the saints, and in the end, if they are truly God's children, they will be willing to do what is necessary to regain the access and favor of the people of God.

Furthermore, if God's children are required to seek forgiveness with one another before they approach God (Matt. 5:23–24), how much more are they required to make things right with His church if they happen to be under its discipline? In this community relationship, what the church binds on earth will be bound in heaven. To be right with God is to be right with His church.

Of course, if a person can be content outside the fellowship and communion of the church and content remaining in his or her sin, then that person has proven not to be a Christian at all (1 John 2:19), and church discipline has proven to be effective in purifying the membership of the church.

Conclusion

The church is not a man-made institution that operates under its own authority and power. Rather, the church is established and governed by Christ. When the church is in line with Scripture, its commission is divine, its doctrine powerful, and its discipline binding. Christians are called to submit to its teaching and discipline, and those who refuse to listen to the church are refusing to listen to God (Luke 10:16). In short, Christ has given power and authority to the church to proclaim and execute His teaching to instruct and hold His people accountable to all that He has commanded.

Review Questions

1. From where does the church get its authority?

2. What is the jurisdiction of church authority?

3. What is church discipline?

4. What is the purpose of church discipline?

5. What should be the attitude of those carrying out church discipline?

6. What are the steps to church discipline?

7. Is church discipline optional for churches?

8. Is church discipline effective? Why or why not?

5

The Offices
of the Church

THE CHURCH IS NOT A CHRISTIAN FAMILY listening to online sermons together at home. The church is not two or three believers meeting at a coffee shop to talk about the Lord. The church is not even a few Christians who regularly gather together for Bible study and prayer.

Listening to sermons at home, fellowshipping with other believers over a cup of coffee, and even attending Bible conferences are all good, but all these things lack the biblical structure, organization, and government that God has required for His church.

There can be no real church without a committed membership, formal accountability, and structured leadership. Such organization is necessary because it has been prescribed for the church by God.

The main organization needed for the church is a plurality of ordained leaders (Titus 1:5). The church is to be governed by its leaders. And according to the Scriptures, the official offices of leadership in the church are twofold: elders and deacons (Phil. 1:1).

Elders must have both an exemplary personal and family life and have been gifted by the Spirit with teaching the Scriptures (1 Tim. 3:2–5). The responsibilities of this office are preaching and teaching, ruling, overseeing the spiritual affairs of the church, and shepherding the souls of those who are under the care of the elders (1 Tim. 3:5; 2 Tim. 4:1–5; 1 Peter 5:1–3).

Deacons, similarly, must have an exemplary personal and family life coupled with a heart to serve God's people (1 Tim. 3:10). Deacons are not called to be janitors, for any member of the church can be responsible for taking out the trash. Rather, deacons are servants who are called to minister to the needs of the saints (Acts 6:3). They are to be an extension of the arms and legs of the elders to assist in the administration and facilitation of church ministry (Acts 6:1–3).

To help the elders guard their study and prayer time, God appointed deacons to handle the requests and needs of the saints (Acts 6:4). Loving and caring and ministering to *people* are the main objectives of deacons, not unlocking the church doors and getting the coffee ready. Their priorities are visiting the sick, attending to the needs of the widows, and caring for troubled and hurting members of the church. Though the responsibilities of deacons may include overseeing the upkeep and maintenance of the church facilities, even these responsibilities have the greater end of serving God's people.

Qualifications for Elders and Deacons

Elders

1. Blameless
2. Husband of one wife
3. Vigilant
4. Sober
5. Good behavior
6. Hospitable
7. Able to teach*
8. Not given to wine
9. Not violent
10. Not greedy
11. Patient
12. Not quarrelsome
13. Not covetous
14. Exemplary in ruling his family
15. Not a novice
16. A good testimony to those outside the church

Deacons

1. Reverent
2. Not double-tongued
3. Not given to much wine
4. Not greedy
5. A pure conscience
6. Tested
7. Blameless
8. Faithful wife
9. Exemplary in ruling his family

Pastors Are Called of God

Sadly, too many men decide to enter the ministry because *pastoring* sounds like a good career opportunity or because they don't have any other good ideas of what they should do with their lives. Even worse, churches are too eager to call these types of pastoral candidates. Churches often choose a new pastor based on his management skills, personality, looks, or charisma rather than on the biblical qualifications of personal godliness, doctrine, and his ability to handle the Word of God. Because of this, churches are full

---

* Note that there is only one essential difference between the office of elder and deacon—the ability to teach.

of unqualified pastors who haven't been spiritually gifted or called of God.

Good preaching that nourishes souls includes both skill and spiritual gifting. A certain level of training and skill is needed to exposit the Word of God properly. It is amazing how many preachers lack the basic knowledge and ability to exegete a passage of Scripture properly and to give application without distorting the intended meaning of the passage. Sadly, many sermons coming from pulpits across the globe do not even come close to being an exposition of Scripture but resemble a self-help motivational speech with a few Bible verses sprinkled in for good measure. Furthermore, the lack of biblical and theological knowledge many of today's pastors have is amazing.

Even more important than natural ability and biblical training, true preaching is accompanied by the super-natural power of the Holy Spirit. Much of today's preaching is lacking in power. Sermons seem more like a discussion than an authoritative word from heaven.

True preaching is recognizable not necessarily by a dynamic and eloquent speech but rather by the Word of God being accurately proclaimed and applied in the power of the Holy Spirit. Churches need clear and precise teaching, not winsome personalities. More than anything else, preaching needs to be biblical and Spirit-empowered—preaching that rebukes, encourages, and edifies the church. When the church hears true preaching, it hears something supernatural—that is, the church hears from God Himself. True preaching is authoritative, corrective, edifying, and ultimately, sanctifying. Preaching with power is a spiritual gifting obtained from God alone.

True ministers have a divine calling and gifting on their lives. At least three identifying marks separate those whom God has called to the ministry from those who have entered the ministry of their own accord:

1. Those called of God have a burning and unquenchable desire to teach and preach God's Word. They have a message from God that they feel compelled to proclaim.

2. Those whom God calls are those who have providential opportunity to preach. This alone does not indicate a man's calling, but it is doubtful that God would call a man into the ministry without providing him an opportunity to minister.

3. Most importantly, the chief confirmation of a man's calling is the verification of the local church. If the church is not consistently hearing from God in a man's preaching, it is not likely that the man has been called by God.

Ordination, which is the official confirmation of the local church that affirms God's calling upon a man, is important for the ministry. If God's people are not spiritually blessed and ministered to by a man's preaching, it is not likely that that man has been gifted or called of God.

Local churches must be careful not to continue to encourage uncalled men to preach because they are afraid to hurt the man's feelings. Also, men should be wary about starting a new church without having their gifts verified by an established church. Too many churches have been started because of the unwillingness of a non-ordained preacher to submit to the judgment of a pre-existing biblical church.

With all this said, not all God's called ministers are gifted equally. All preachers are unique and have different strengths and weaknesses. The church needs to be careful not to be too critical and judgmental of their pastor. We must not judge and compare our pastor with our favorite celebrity preacher. This was the error of the Corinthians as they argued who the better preacher was—Paul or Apollos. It is fine to have a favorite preacher, but we are on dangerous ground when we make one particular preacher the standard for all other preachers to meet. The quickest way to cease hearing the voice of God in our pastor's preaching is to start listening with a critical spirit.

Pastors Are Called to Shepherd

Pastors are not called to be CEOs of a corporation; they are called to be shepherds of God's sheep. The church is not a business, and thus, pastors should not seek to operate the church as a business. More is required of pastors than dynamic leadership and effective communication skills. The man of God is called foremost to be familiar with God's presence through fervent prayer and consistent study of His Word. If pastors are not regularly on their knees and committed to the study of the truth, no matter how gifted they may be, they will be poor spiritual guides. They may succeed in building a business, but they will fail at overseeing and caring for God's church. Leadership skills are one thing; pastoring is quite another. In part, pastoring includes serving, preaching, counseling, and living an exemplary life for others to follow.

Pastors Are Called to Serve

Pastors are servants. Pastoring a church is a ministry, not a career, and so pastors must never place themselves or their ministry above God's sheep. Pastors must sacrifice their personal aspirations for greatness, do away with the desire to become a Christian celebrity, and be willing (if need be) to minister in obscurity. They are not to use smaller churches as stepping stones to gain the employment of bigger churches. Pastoring is not about building a resumé, for God's sheep are not to be exploited in this fashion. Just as shepherds are not to leave the sheep when danger approaches (John 10:11–13), pastors are not to abandon their flock just because the opportunity to minister in greener pastures becomes available. Instead, God's ministers should be willing to sacrifice and give themselves to feeding, ministering, and serving God's sheep wherever God may call them. The needs and care of the flock should always come first (Acts 20:28; 1 Peter 5:1–3).

Pastoring is not about money or prestige but about watching over God's heritage (1 Peter 5:2–3). Pastors are to walk beside the sheep, pray for the sheep, preach to the sheep, rebuke the sheep, and encourage the sheep as needed. This takes humility, godliness, meekness, and patience, which come only by walking daily in the Spirit (Gal. 5:22–25). If pastors are not willing to serve, they are not fit ministers of God's people.

In short, pastoring is about giving, not receiving, and it is about ministering to and not exploiting God's people. Good pastors, therefore, are those who are more concerned about the praise of God than the praise of men. God gives pastors to serve the church rather than giving the church to serve pastors.

Pastors Are Called to Preach

Pastors must give themselves to doctrine (1 Tim. 4:13–16), for they are called to labor in the Word (1 Tim. 5:17; Titus 1:9). The principal task of pastors is to feed God's sheep; the principal calling of a pastor is preaching and teaching (John 21:15; 1 Tim. 4:15–16; 2 Tim. 4:1–5). "The first and principal duty of a pastor," according to John Owen, "is to feed the flock by diligent preaching of the word."[1] Owen also states, "He is no pastor who doth not feed his flock."[2] Pastors must, therefore, study to show themselves approved of God and be able to interpret rightly and apply the truth (2 Tim. 2:15). Since pastors are called to preach, they must be committed students of God's Word.

---

1 John Owen, "The True Nature of a Gospel Church and Its Government," in *The Works of John Owen: The Church and the Bible*, ed. William H. Goold (Edinburgh: Banner of Truth, 1991), 16:74.

2 John Owen, "The Duty of a Pastor," in *The Works of John Owen: Sermons to the Church*, ed. William H. Goold (Edinburgh: Banner of Truth, 1991), 9:453.

When it comes to the studying of the Scriptures, laziness should not characterize the man of God. Thus, pastors should be found most often in their study, drawing close to God, rather than on the golf course rubbing shoulders with the prominent leaders of the community. If pastors are not ready at all times to preach, they are neglecting one of their principal responsibilities.

Pastors Are Called to Counsel

Pastors are to comfort, rebuke, correct, encourage, and instruct those who are in spiritual need. To be effective in biblical counseling, pastors must first visit with God before they visit with others. They must receive counsel from the Scriptures before they become competent to counsel others. Counseling is to come from the overflow of a heart that has been saturated with the Word of God.

Pastors Are Called to Live Exemplary Lives

One of the more impressive qualities of the apostle Paul was his exemplary life as a Christian. With the guidance of the Spirit, he could boldly proclaim, "Follow me as I follow Christ" (1 Cor. 11:1; Phil. 3:17). Paul lived out his doctrine and provided a visible illustration of his message in his life. In the same way, pastors are called to live an exemplary Christian life for their congregation to follow. If they are going to preach the Word, they must live out that Word. The best compliment that can be said about any pastor is that he is a godly man completely committed to what he teaches.

Pastors Are Called to Rule

A pastor is one among a plurality of pastors and elders who are to watch and govern over the flock of God (Titus 1:5). A plurality of elders is a natural safeguard against many dangers. Having multiple elders prevents blame from being pinpointed on a single person.

A plurality of leaders can use their different strengths to be more productive and balanced in their leadership.

Pastors Are Called to Submit

Pastors are leaders, but they are to be a part of a plurality of elders that submit to each other and are held in check by the congregation. It is not wise for any one leader, apart from Christ Jesus, to be without accountability.

Conclusion

There are only two ordained offices in the church: deacons and elders. Both are called to serve and minister to the flock of God, with elders given the special responsibilities to teach and preach and rule. Together, these two offices are sufficient to minister to and oversee the church of the living God.

Review Questions

1. What are the two offices of the church?

2. Why is a plurality of leaders helpful?

3. What are the two main passages of Scripture that list the qualifications of church leaders?

4. Why is godliness so important for church leaders?

5. What is the key difference between the two offices of the church?

6. What are the responsibilities of deacons?

7. Why are preaching and teaching the main responsibilities of the elders?

6

The Government
of the Church

WHO IS IN CHARGE? Of course, Christ is the head of the church, but who makes all the important decisions, such as picking out the color of the new carpet for the sanctuary? Are decisions made by a majority vote of the congregation, or do the elders make all the decisions? In this chapter, we will see that the Bible has given the oversight of the church to a plurality of elders who are accountable to the church body.

The Separation of Power

Christ, as the sole head of the church, does not delegate power exclusively to the elders or to the congregation. Rather, Christ gives certain authority to the elders, and He gives certain authority to the congregation. The elders have authority to teach, administer the ordinances, call special meetings, oversee, and rule, while the congregation has authority to appoint and dismiss their elders, accept new members, and discipline and discharge disorderly members.

The elders and the congregation receive their respective authority not from each other but directly and immediately from Christ—the head of the church. For instance, the responsibilities of the elders are derived from the authority of Christ, not from the authority of the congregation. Yes, elders are to be held accountable by the congregation, but their duties are given to them by Christ. In like manner, the elders do not have the right to take away any of the privileges and responsibilities that Christ has directly delegated to the congregation.

The Responsibility and Authority of Elders

Elders rule by the delegated authority of Scripture. The extent or jurisdiction of their authority is restricted to the spiritual affairs of the church. Elders do not have the authority to manage the private affairs of the congregation any more than an employer has the authority to tell an employee what to do on his or her time off. God does hold the elders accountable for watching over the congregation's spiritual lives and the overall direction of the church. Elders are not to lord over God's heritage (1 Peter 5:3). Yet, just as parents cannot vacate their responsibility to rule over their children by placing their children in charge, elders are not free to place the congregation in charge.

No doubt, wise and loving parents listen to the concerns and desires of their children; in the same way, elders need to listen to the general concerns, wisdom, and thoughts of their congregation. It is wise to bring the non-doctrinal and practical decisions, such as relocations or building projects, to the congregation for corporate prayer with the desire for collective agreement and unity. In the end, God holds elders to a greater accountability, for they have been given the responsibility and authority to teach and rule over the household of God (1 Tim. 3:5).

The Responsibility of Members

God commands church members to "obey your leaders and submit to them, for they are keeping watch over your souls, as those who will have to give an account. Let them do this with joy and not with groaning, for that would be of no advantage to you" (Heb. 13:17). Therefore, the congregation should never seek to operate without the knowledge, consent, and leadership of their elders.

Yet, the increasing mind-set of many church members is an attitude of self-sufficiency. It seems that a growing number of Christians feel as if their spiritual life is no one else's business. These Christians seem to think that the elders of their church have no business prying into their lives by giving them spiritual counsel or correction.

It is one thing for church members to hold their elders accountable; it's quite another for church members to place their independent judgment relating to church life above the leadership of the church. If many of today's Christians do not agree with a decision of the elders, they will protest, even boycott the church and stay at home, to show their displeasure. Too many Christians feel they can take what they like and leave what they don't like about a church. These types of Christians place their personal judgment above the judgment of the church's leadership.

How many churches have split, or new churches formed, because of power and control issues rather than because of legitimate and biblical concerns? It is sad to learn about Christians who seem to love the Lord keeping their families at home on Sunday mornings because they are unable to find a local church that they agree with on every little issue of church life. Even more troubling is when these men, who have never proven to be submissive to others, seek to start their own church.

I am afraid that much of what is behind the rising *home-church* movement, where the role of ordained elders is minimized or even removed, is an attitude against submission. There is nothing wrong with a church meeting in a home, but removing the role and authority of elders undermines the authority of the church. The home-church movement, so it seems, is most attractive and appealing to those who are resistant to any form of personal accountability. The real problem with this attitude is a lack of submission to Christ. Christ Jesus is the one who organized and gifted the church with its offices of leadership and then called His people to come under their delegated oversight and authority.

The Authority of Members

Elders have authority, but it is not absolute authority. The congregation has a measure of authority as well. Each church member has been given authority by Christ in at least five areas:

1. *Affirming New Members*

All new members are to be affirmed by the church when admitted to membership. For instance, before the church in Jerusalem accepted Saul, it was important for them to learn of his conversion (Acts 9:26–27). While church membership cannot be denied the weakest believer who has a credible profession of faith and is walking in obedience, the congregation must have an opportunity to protest any membership candidate who they know is living an openly scandalous life.

2. *Choosing Their Own Leaders*

Not only does the congregation have the authority to affirm new members, they have the authority to affirm their own leaders (Acts 6:3–5). Neither the state nor a parachurch organization has the right to install church leaders. This right belongs to each local church (Acts 14:23).

3. *Holding Their Leaders Accountable*

Members are responsible for submitting to their elders, but members are also responsible for holding their elders accountable to God's Word. *Guarding the truth* is every member's responsibility. Because elders are recognized and approved by the congregation, the congregation has the authority to appoint their own leaders as well as remove those from office who no longer meet the biblical qualifications that God requires of them (1 Tim. 3:1–7).

Elders who stray doctrinally or ethically must be subjected to the discipline that God has given to the church body. Elders are members of the church too, and no member is exempt from accountability. They, like every other member, are not excused from church discipline (1 Tim. 5:19).

Congregations cannot neglect this responsibility either. Church members who tolerate unorthodoxy, ethical scandal, or abusiveness in their leadership will be held accountable by God. That is, God places culpability for the rise of false teachers upon the congregants who have itching ears (2 Tim. 4:3).

4. *Holding Members Accountable*

Church members have the authority to hold each other accountable as well. Though there are distinct roles between elders and members (one leads, and the other follows), they have the same objective (to uphold the unity, purity, and verity of the church), and they have the same basic tasks (to love, edify, care for, and watch over one another in the Lord). Pastors are called to lead the flock, and the flock is called to follow the teaching and example of their pastors. Pastors are called to teach the members to do the work of the ministry (Eph. 4:12).

Pastors are not only called to watch and care for God's flock, but also to equip the flock to watch and care for each other. Pastors care for people from a leadership position and a more visible platform, while members care for people discretely from the pew. Though having different roles and different degrees of authority, pastors and members are mutually *accountable* to one another, as they are both called to watch, rebuke, edify, and care for each other.

This means that the authority of the church reaches every member. Though we may like to think that our beliefs and practices are no one else's business, this is simply not the case in biblical Christianity. As with every believer, we are called to be a member of a local church. Being a member of a local church requires that we submit to the care and oversight of its elders and submit to the care and oversight of its members.

5. *Exercising Church Discipline*

Finally, for members to have the authority to hold their elders and themselves accountable, they must have power. This power is *church discipline*. Though additional witnesses are needed for each progressive step of the disciplinary process, a single member has the right and power to initiate the first step of church discipline—*private confrontation*.

The authority given to the congregation to carry out church discipline goes even beyond the authority invested in its elders. Church leaders are not free to carry out the final step of discipline alone. Though private confront-ation can be carried out by a single elder or an individual member, excommunication is performed by the congregation (1 Cor. 5:4–5).

Because church discipline lies with the power of the local body, the local church is autonomous. Because it is impossible for a local congregation to discipline non-members, it is unbiblical for a local church to be governed by non-members, such as an outside board of consultants or a presbytery of men. The authority of the church to govern itself lies within the local assembly. In short, church members are not required to submit to earthly leaders they have no authority or ability to discipline. Thus, the church, with its elders and members, has the authority to carry out its responsibility to oversee and rule itself under the headship of Christ. What a responsibility— but what a blessing that God has given His people as they are called to collectively submit to each other as unto the Lord.

Conclusion

In conclusion, Scripture calls every Christian to submit to one another. Even if we, as individual Christians, have greater wisdom and more spiritual maturity than the elders of our church, as long as our elders do not abuse their delegated power by contradicting the clear teachings of Scripture, we are called to submit and support the decisions of the church. It takes more grace, love, and humility to submit and support the elders of a church than to stand firm on our particular opinions. And hopefully, the color of the carpet is not nearly as important as the beauty of the brethren dwelling together in unity (Ps. 133:1).

How beautiful and sweet it is to see elders rule in accordance with the principles of Scripture in the spirit of humility and love and to see the congregation collectively seeking to be supportive and submissive to the rule and authority of the church. Oh, that God would grant His church the grace to live out this divine and biblical model of church life!

Review Questions

1. What are the two branches of power within the local church?

2. From where do the elders derive their power?

3. Who holds the elders accountable?

4. Are elders above church discipline?

5. What power and responsibilities are given to the elders?

6. What power and responsibilities are given to the congregation?

7. Why is church discipline given to the congregation?

Part 3

The Purpose
of the Church

Go therefore and make disciples of all nations, baptizing them in the name of the Father and of the Son and of the Holy Spirit, teaching them to observe all that I have commanded you. And behold, I am with you always, to the end of the age.

— Matthew 28:19-20

7

The Mission
of the Church

THERE IS A LOT OF CONFUSION about the purpose of the church. Does the church exist to feed and clothe the poor and homeless? Does the church exist to bring about cosmic restoration and political reform to our society? Does the church exist to combat social injustices and inequalities? Sure, the church exists to preach the gospel, but what about these other objectives?

To answer these questions, it is important for us to examine three things. First, we need to have a basic understanding of biblical theology so we can properly assess the role the church plays in carrying out God's purpose on earth in the history of redemption. Second, we must examine the nature of the church so we can understand why the church exists in the first place. Third, we need to observe the mission statement Christ issued to the church so we can understand its purpose. In short, we need to understand (1) the role the church plays in the history of redemption, (2) the nature of the church, and (3) the Great Commission.

The History of Redemption

To begin with, we need to have a fundamental understanding of biblical theology and the role the church plays in the story line of redemption.

Two Ages and Two Kingdoms

From a big-picture perspective, in the history of redemption there are two stages, or ages: *this present evil age* and *the age to come* (Gal. 1:4; Eph. 1:21). This present evil age, according to Scripture, spans from the fall of Adam until the return of Christ (Matt. 28:20). It is depicted as the time period in which darkness, bondage, unrighteousness, and death reign over the earth. According to Jesus, all unbelievers are born into this fallen world as "children of this age" (Luke 20:34), and according to Paul, the children of this age are held captive to the power of this age (Gal. 1:4-5). This present evil age, consequently, is the reign of the kingdom of darkness over the people, the governments, and the nations of this world (Rev. 18:3).

This present evil age and the kingdom of darkness will not pass away until the return of Christ, for only when Christ returns will *the age to come* arrive. The age to come is when the "new heavens and a new earth in which righteousness dwells" is established (2 Peter 3:13). Only then, at the physical return of Christ, will this fallen world pass away with fire, and only then will the eternal state of glory be established on the new resurrected earth. This means that cosmic restoration will not take place until "creation itself will be set free from its bondage to corruption and obtain the freedom of the glory of the children of God" (Rom. 8:21).

The age to come is the eternal state when light, life, and liberty will reign forever. The age to come is the kingdom of heaven. And though the kingdom of heaven is not established on earth (during this present evil age), its power is currently manifested on the earth within the church (Titus 2:11–13). That is, those who have been united, by faith, to the King of Glory have "tasted the goodness of the word of God and the powers of the age to come" (Heb. 6:5). They have been delivered from the domain and kingdom of darkness and transferred into the kingdom of God's dear Son (Col. 1:13). By being born again by the Spirit, they have entered the kingdom of heaven.

Thus, during this present evil age, the kingdom of heaven is invisible to the unbelieving world as it exists only within the minds and hearts of believers (Luke 17:20–21; John 18:36). Believers have been given the first fruits of the age to come as they have entered the kingdom of heaven and been given eternal life in the Son.

The Church and the Kingdom of Heaven

Consequently, the power of the kingdom of heaven is *already* present within the church *but not yet* manifested over the kingdoms of this world. The world knows nothing of the life, power, freedom, and peace of the kingdom of heaven. The nations and rulers of this age remain in darkness and under the dominion of Satan.

For this reason, those in the church are pilgrims and strangers in this fallen world (1 Peter 2:11). Christians are foreigners and exiles on this earth (Heb. 11:13). As citizens of heaven, they have not placed their hope in this present world, which is passing away (1 John 2:17), but in an everlasting kingdom, "whose designer and builder is God" (Heb. 11:10). In this sense, the church, as the household of God, functions as the embassy of the kingdom of heaven on earth.

Yes, every square inch of this universe belongs to Christ, but not all of it has bowed the knee to Christ. Though Christ sovereignly rules over Satan and the kingdoms of this world, His Word is only embraced and followed by those inside the embassy of heaven.

Only those within the church have submitted to His lordship. Only those within the church have His protection from the wrath to come. Only those inside the church have found peace and liberty under His leadership. Only those in the church, by faith, have seen the kingdom of God (John 3:3). Only the church has experienced the liberating power of the age to come. Thus, the kingdom of heaven, in this present evil age, will not expand beyond those united by faith to the King—the church.

The Two Kingdoms are Incompatible

Like oil and water, the kingdom of darkness and the kingdom of heaven are incompatible. Light and darkness have nothing in common (2 Cor. 6:14). It is impossible, therefore, to merge these two opposing kingdoms. Civil magistrates have no jurisdiction over the embassy of heaven, and the church has no business carrying out its mission by the use of the earthly weapons of this world (2 Cor. 10:4). Just as Christ did not attempt to establish His kingdom through political force (John 18:36), the church should not be deceived into thinking it can expand God's kingdom through political and social revolutions. Political marches, protests, rallies, and activism are not the keys to the kingdom of heaven.

The best that earthly governments can do, even if they are led by Christians, is to restrain evil and punish evildoers (1 Peter 2:14). Yet, such political measures have no power to break the chains of darkness and liberate the children of this age from the power of sin. The theocracy of the Jewish state, in the Old Testament, proved that even the best legislation cannot establish the kingdom of heaven on earth. Though political power may influence external behavior for the good, it cannot undo the kingdom of darkness that lies within the hearts of those enslaved to the ruler of this present evil age.

The Keys and Mission of the Church

The only hope for this world is the gospel message that has been entrusted to the embassy of heaven. For this reason, the mission of the church is not the restoration of this present evil age by social reforms and legislative laws. The kingdom of heaven is not advanced by such means.

Don't misunderstand me. Every individual Christian, as he or she remains an active member of society, is called to personally help those in need, pray for their rulers, and do what they can to promote justice and equality in this present evil age. Although Christians are not of this world, they remain in this world (John 15:19; 17:14-19). The Word of God does impact how Christians live in this world. They have their civic duties, such as voting their conscience and paying their taxes (Matt. 22:21). They are called by God to help their neighbors who are in need (Prov. 3:27–28) and have compassion for the sick, poor, and opposed of this world. They are to seek to do good to all. Wherever Christianity goes, such blessings are sure to follow.

Yet the responsibilities of individual Christians and the blessings that follow the spread of the gospel are not the same thing as the Great Commission that Christ has given to the church as a society of believers. The church is not called to take control of the nations. It is not even called to feed the nations. God has not promised to sanctify the culture or redeem earthly governments. Earl Blackburn rightly assesses the problem:

> Today, many believe the primary purposes of the church are to feed the poor, to educate the illiterate, to teach the underprivileged and underdeveloped nations how to farm, build homes, and establish welfare systems, and to promote liberation from tyrannical governments. This is called the "social gospel." While there is a legitimate need for many of these activities in the world today, these are not the church's primary responsibilities. The "social gospel" is not the gospel at all; it can be used as a subtle device of Satan to sidetrack true churches of God from their main purpose.[1]

---

1 Earl M. Blackburn, *Jesus Loves the Church and So Should You* (Birmingham, AL: Solid Ground Christian Books, 2010), 43.

And the main purpose and mission of the church is preaching the gospel. The only way the church can carry out its mission and advance the kingdom of heaven is by wielding the power of the gospel (Rom. 1:16). The keys to the kingdom of heaven are not social activism and world domination but the message of forgiveness in Jesus Christ.

The church has been entrusted with these keys for a reason. Only by unleashing the powers of the age to come through the preaching of the Word of God will the children of this present evil age be delivered from the bondage of darkness and the ruler of this world. Only by the spread of the gospel will the kingdom of heaven expand across the globe to those who believe. The kingdom of heaven will not advance any other way.

The church is called to rescue sinners from this present evil age by bringing the power and blessings of the age to come to those, and only those, who surrender their lives to the King of heaven. At Christ's glorious return, all creation will be restored as the glory and the knowledge of God will cover the earth as water covers the sea (Hab. 2:14). When the kingdom of heaven is filled with a redeemed people from every nation and tongue and tribe of people, then the work and mission of the church will be finished. Then, and only then, will the "kingdom of the world . . . become the kingdom of our Lord and of his Christ, and he shall reign forever and ever" (Rev. 11:15).

Until then, in this present evil age, the church needs to make sure it does not become distracted and lay aside the only power it has to effect real change in this fallen world—the gospel of Jesus Christ.

The Nature of the Church

Not only does the story line of the history of redemption shed light on the mission of the church, the nature of the church indicates its mission as well. As hammers, staplers, pens, and other such tools and instruments are made to do what they were designed to do, the church is called to do what God has made it to be. As Earl Blackburn states: "The existence and nature of the church cannot be separated from its purpose."[2]

With this in mind, the church was established by the Lord to worship and glorify God by proclaiming the gospel to the world and by being the steward of the means of the sanctification of the saints through the upholding and propagating of God's Word. Paul explains in Ephesians 4:9–16 that the church has three distinct objectives: (1) to maintain its intrinsic *unity* in Christ by functioning as an interdependent community, (2) by growing in *purity* in the pursuit of personal and corporate holiness, (3) and through standing firm in believing and proclaiming the *truth*.

Each objective is not only tied to the other but each also aids in the performance of the other. When maturing in these three areas (unity, purity, and verity), the church glorifies God when it follows its purpose. What is the purpose of the church? To be what God made it to be—a united and holy people who uphold, follow, and propagate the truth of God's Word in an uncompromising fashion.

1. The Church Is to Grow in Unity

According to the Scriptures, the church is a unified body of believers, and their inherent unity needs to be fostered and lived out in the everyday functions of the church. It is through unity that the church is called to function as a community of individuals who fellowship and work together for the mutual edification of the whole.

We learn in Ephesians 4:9–16 that God has given the church spiritual leaders for equipping the saints for the work of the ministry. Thus, it is a mistake to think that the ministry belongs exclusively to the elders and teachers of the church. As ministers

---

2 Blackburn, *Jesus Loves the Church*, 43.

equip the congregants, they, in turn, are enabled to minister to one another. Paul goes on to stress the necessity of the universal ministry of the body of Christ: "From whom the whole body, joined and held together by every joint with which it is equipped, when each part is working properly, makes the body grow so that it builds itself up in love" (Eph. 4:16).

Our church community must consist of this heartfelt fellowship and cooperation of the saints. The church is to be a family, where church members help, pray, exhort, rebuke, and encourage one another in love. Therefore, when one member suffers or rejoices, the rest of the church suffers or rejoices as well. In this way, each church member is called "to walk in a manner worthy of the calling to which [they] have been called, with all humility and gentleness, with patience, bearing with one another in love, eager to maintain the unity of the Spirit in the bond of peace" (Eph. 4:1–3).

If the church is one in Christ, with no distinctions between ethnicity, gender, and social class, and if the church is called to function as a community in love, then the church needs to be mindful of practical ways to cultivate community within the church body.

To maintain unity, the church must guard against subtle forms of segregation within the congregation by primarily associating with those of the same age or personal interests. Forming cliques discourages interaction and fellowship between young married couples, youth, senior citizens, and so forth. Instead, the church should encourage the young to learn from the older saints, and likewise, the elders of the church need to be willing to teach the younger. As with family functions, there may be a proper time for our children to go outside and play together, but when it comes time to eat or learn, let us drink and break bread together as a family under the headship of Christ.

We the church must encourage fellowship not only during organized functions but also in the homes of the congregants (by families and individuals spontaneously getting together). In fact, much of the ministry of the church should occur outside the Sunday morning worship service in living rooms, dining rooms, and the backyards of the families of the church.

In gist, rather than gravitating toward a disconnected, isolated, and once-a-week Sunday morning worship experience, the church is to proactively and intentionally foster a sense of community among believers that extends both inside and outside the walls of the church building.

2. The Church Is to Grow in Purity

The church body functioning within its purpose will be a means of sanctification for the people of God. The goal is for the church to be individually and collectively molded into the perfect image and stature of the Lord Jesus Christ (Eph. 4:13). "The local church," therefore, according to Don Kistler, "is God's tool for bringing His people to full maturity in knowledge and faith."[3] Christ's objective for the church has always been "that he might present the church to himself in splendor, without spot or wrinkle or any such thing, that she might be holy and without blemish" (Eph. 5:27). Consequently, sin and worldliness need to be confronted as we strive for holiness. This pursuit restricts the membership of the church to believers only, and it requires church discipline when needed among its members.

3. The Church Is to Grow in the Knowledge of the Truth

Since the church is the pillar and ground of the truth, its members must give their energy to upholding, following, and propagating the truth.

First, how should the church go about *upholding* the truth? If God's Word is absolute, unchanging, and authoritative, then the

---

3 Don Kistler, "Blest Be the Tie That Binds" in *Onward Christian Soldiers*, ed. Don Kistler (Morgan, PA. Soli Deo Gloria, 1999), 98.

church is called to proclaim it as such. Perhaps there has never been a time in history when the church has been so tempted to make theological compromises. God's people are to hold fast to the faith in such times. Whenever a local church waters down the truth or neglects certain aspects of it for the sake of gaining a larger hearing or for any other reason, it has lost its way. The church has denied itself and its leader, Jesus Christ, when it places numerical growth above fulfilling its divine purpose.

Second, Christ not only commissioned the church to uphold the truth, He called it to *grow* in the truth and in the knowledge of the Lord. That is, the church is called to be sanctified by the truth (John 17:17). Paul fleshes this out in Ephesians 4:11–14:

> And he gave the apostles, the prophets, the evangelists, the [pastors] and teachers, to equip the saints for the work of ministry, for building up the body of Christ, until we all attain to the unity of the faith and of the knowledge of the Son of God, to mature manhood, to the measure of the stature of the fullness of Christ, so that we may no longer be children, tossed to and fro by the waves and carried about by every wind of doctrine, by human cunning, by craftiness in deceitful schemes.

According to this passage, the truth is both vital for safeguarding the church from doctrinal error and for bringing about spiritual maturity in the body of Christ. Thus, the church should never be ashamed of sound doctrine nor shy away from teaching the whole counsel of God (Acts 20:27).

Third, God commissioned the church to *spread* the truth to those within the walls of the church as well as to those outside the church. One of the chief goals of the church is to evangelize and make disciples for Christ (Matt. 28:19). The church is not only responsible for preaching the gospel to those in attendance on Sunday morning but also for equipping the saints to be ready to do personal evangelism on Monday morning. Every Christian needs to clearly understand the gospel message (especially the doctrine of justification by faith alone) and then be competent to share his or her faith with family, friends, and neighbors (1 Peter 3:15). The Lord Jesus did not entrust His church with silver or gold; He entrusted it with the truth. Thus, it is the truth that the church is responsible for disseminating to all people. The church is the light of the world; for this reason, it is imperative for church members to be active in evangelism in the local community and in supporting world missions.

This leads us to the third means of ascertaining the purpose of the church—the mission statement that Christ prescribed to the church in Matthew 28.

The Great Commission

The mission of the church is not only affirmed by the role it plays in the story line of redemption and its threefold nature of unity, purity, and verity but also in the mission statement that Christ personally prescribed to the church. Consequently, the Great Commission and the purpose of the church are the same.

The objective of the church does not merely consist of evangelism. The church's mission is to make disciples. This includes evangelizing unbelievers, but it also consists of teaching the whole counsel of God's Word to believers. Spreading the gospel to the world is a vital part of fulfilling the Great Commission, but so is preaching in the pulpit each Sunday to believers.

The church's commission is not complete until it has taught everything that Christ has instructed it to teach. Not only are we to go into all the world, when we get there we are to teach them to observe all that Christ has commanded. Simply put, the commission of the church consists of proclaiming the whole counsel of God to the saints and preaching the gospel to the world (Matt. 28:18–20).

Discipling Believers

The Great Commission has everything to do with spreading and upholding the truth in a world that wants to suppress it. We cannot evangelize our communities or carry out world missions without seeking to plant churches throughout the world. The goal of the Great Commission is not simply to rescue people from hell but to make disciples of Christ. And discipleship, according to God's plan, is to be carried out in the local church. Paul wasn't content to preach the gospel and see sinners converted only to leave them to themselves. His missionary efforts were not complete until churches were planted and elders were established (Titus 1:5). The objective, for this reason, is to evangelize the lost and equip the saints to follow Christ in every area of their lives (Eph. 4:11).

The church has the responsibility to preach the gospel and disciple believers in their communities. Though it is shortsighted to be self-focused, the church's main priority is to disciple its people. The idea that the church is no longer about "us" once we become Christians is unbiblical, to say the least.

The church is for believers because the church is to consist of believers. The local church should be principally concerned with building up its own members. Maturity and holiness are the goals. If the church fails here, it fails everywhere. If the church does not care for its members, it has no business seeking to reach those on the other side of the world.

Evangelizing Unbelievers

Yet, the church does have the responsibility of evangelizing the lost. Christ has called us all to be fishers of men (Matt. 4:19). We are called to be the salt of the earth and a light on a hill (Matt. 5:13–14). The church making no new disciples is a sure way for the gates of hell to prevail in the next generation.

However, saying evangelism is the church's respon-sibility is not saying that the local church is required to have an organized outreach program. The responsibility to evangelize falls on every church member. To reach the community, a church doesn't have to run community outreach events but only encourage and equip its members to be ready to give an answer to those who ask for the reason for the hope they have in Christ (1 Peter 3:15).

If the church wants to evangelize its community, then the church can do nothing better than teach its members a clear and precise gospel. The church is to equip and encourage Christ's disciples to evangelize. Every Christian should know the basic gospel message and the doctrine of justification by faith alone. Understanding God's sovereignty in salvation is also important when it comes to evangelism. If the church fails to teach these core doctrines, then the church is failing at the Great Commission.

Missions Begin at Home

Evangelism begins with those who are closest to us. We are to love our neighbors, and that begins with those who are nearest to us— our lost family members. Our children need the gospel. If we are unconcerned about their salvation, why would we be concerned about the children of the Aborigines in the unreached corners of the world? Charles Spurgeon was adamant about this:

> The heathen are to be sought by all means, and the highways and hedges are to be searched, but home has a prior claim, and woe unto those who reverse the order of the Lord's arrangements. . . . Parental teaching is a natural duty—who so fit to look to the child's well-being as those who are the authors of his actual being? To neglect the instruction of our offspring is worse than brutish.[4]

---

4 Charles H. Spurgeon, *Morning and Evening*, rev. and updated by Alistair Begg (Wheaton, IL: Crossway, 2003), Evening, July 11.

Missions begin with parenting. The principal goal of parenting is not to raise obedient children and productive citizens. It is something much more serious—something impossible. Only the Lord can save our children, but we have the privilege and responsibility to point them to Christ.

The church is responsible for teaching parents about biblical parenting. Churches must encourage family worship in the home. Discipling our children's hearts must be our chief priority when it comes to missions.

Missions Extend to Our Communities

Missions begin in the home but should flow over into the streets of our neighborhoods. Every Christian is a missionary; every Christian is to be an evangelist. We are not all equally gifted or as outgoing as others, but we are all called to be a light. Whether we are comfortable reaching out to strangers or feel more suited speaking a timely word to friends, we must be purposeful about sharing the gospel with others. Let us never be ashamed of Christ! As Christ said: "For whoever is ashamed of me and of my words in this adulterous and sinful generation, of him will the Son of Man also be ashamed when he comes in the glory of his Father with the holy angels" (Mark 8:38).

Missions End at the Four Corners of the Globe

The desire of the early church should be the desire of the modern church. The early church was not content with only reaching Jerusalem with the gospel. In just a few years, the gospel traveled throughout the known world. The ultimate objective is rescuing a people for God out of every people, tribe, race, and nation.

Missions Should Not Be Separated from the Church

To separate missions from the church is to misunderstand the Great Commission. Missions are the responsibility of the church.

The local church sends out missionaries, and these missionaries seek to plant local churches.

It is wrong for Christians to seek to be foreign missionaries without first being submitted to a local church. Sadly, there are too many self-called missionaries who refuse to be submitted to or sent by a local church. They desire the financial support of local churches but not their oversight. In addition, until a local church can be planted in an unreached region and its leadership established, missionaries are to be accountable to their sending churches. Foreign missions should flow out of the local church and be aimed at starting new local churches.

Churches should desire to support and send out missionaries, but missionaries, like the apostle Paul, should be committed to evangelizing the lost and planting churches to disciple those whom the Lord graciously saves. Paul commended the church at Philippi for supporting his missionary efforts (Phil. 4:15). Though the church at Philippi was not rich, they sought to do what they could to advance the kingdom beyond the reach of their city.

Paul did not work in regions where there was already a thriving church; he sought to go where there was no gospel witness at all. Foreign missionaries are needed in the unreached regions of the world. We must either go (Matt. 18:19), or we must send (support) those who do go (Rom. 10:15). Since planting churches is the objective, it seems wisest to support and train indigenous pastors where true churches already exist. It does not make sense to send missionaries to places that already have healthy churches. Rather, why not support those churches and pastors that already have a foothold in those regions? Indigenous pastors have many advantages—they already know the language, do not need to take extended furloughs, and likely will not be leaving the area after four to eight years.

The church has been given a great responsibility. Though reaching the nations seems impossible, the church has been given a promise: "And behold, I am with you always, to the end of the age" (Matt. 28:20). So, no matter what size congregation, the church has no excuse not to make missions a priority.

The aim of the church and the goal of missions is the glory of God. Our concern for lost humanity should drive us to share the gospel, but our love for God should cause our hearts to burn with great desire to see the name of Christ glorified among the nations. Oh, that Christ's name would be praised by every nation and tribe! Oh, that Christ's name would be glorified in our homes, glorified in our communities, and glorified in the four corners of the world! Oh, that Christ would be glorified in the church!

Conclusion

Therefore, according to the history of redemption, the nature of the church, and the Great Commission, the church is to function as an embassy of heaven that grows in unity, purity, and knowledge by coming together for fellowship, mutual edification, and instruction through the explanation and application of the Holy Scriptures as it reproduces itself by taking the gospel to its lost family members, community, and the uttermost parts of the world.

Review Questions

1. What is the mission of the church?

2. What are the keys to the kingdom?

3. Who received the keys to the kingdom—(1) the elders or (2) the congregation or (3) the congregation including the elders?

4. How does being entrusted with the gospel shape the purpose of the church?

5. How do the three marks of the church (unity, purity, and verity) shape the purpose of the church?

6. What is the main objective of the Great Commission?

7. How should the mission of the church shape the activities of the church?

8. Is the church free to create its own purpose?

9. Why do missions begin at home?

10. Why is family worship important?

11. Who is responsible for evangelizing?

12. Why should international missions be sent out of the local church?

13. Why should missionaries seek to establish new local churches?

8

The Methodology
of the Church

THE CHIEF AND SOLE GOAL of the church is to bring glory to God. Yet, glorifying God cannot happen without holiness, and holiness cannot exist apart from the truth. It was for this purpose that the Lord established the church—to glorify God by being a means of evangelizing the lost and sanctifying the saints through the truth.

Since the church is God's holy and united people who have been entrusted with the truth, positionally, it follows, then, that God is only asking the church to be what it is, practically. It would be out of step, for instance, for the church to seek to redefine itself in a desire to increase its influence and acceptability in the world. Instead, the church is called to be itself and live out its very nature in a dark, hostile, and unholy world. Practically speaking, the church is not to be influenced and shaped *by* the culture but to be a sanctifying influence *on* the culture.

It is at this very point—the way the church engages the culture—that the church is tempted to abandon its purpose. The Bible is clear that the church is holy and is called to be holy and the world is unholy and will always be unholy. The culture of the world is shaped by its values—the things of the flesh—while the culture of the church is shaped by its values—the things of the Spirit.

Because Christians live in both spheres (the kingdom of God and the kingdom of this world), there will be some overlap in the cultural activities that the Christian enjoys (e.g., music, language, food, dress). But when the church forgets that the leading influences on the secular culture are worldly values and that the values of the world are in opposition to the spiritual values of the church, it will not be long before the church will be shaped by the values of the world. When the church begins to be swayed by the values of the world and forgets the distinction between holiness and worldliness, it will soon forget its purpose. And if the line between a holy church and the secular world is blurred, undoubtedly the church becomes anthropocentric (man centered) rather than Christo-centric (Christ centered).

Minimizing the Holiness of the Church

Churches often begin this journey away from God by compromising their pursuit of holiness for the sake of broadening their impact and influence on society. This is not to say that influencing culture is a bad objective, but it is an objective that must never trump its main objective. Why? Because once reaching man is more of a concern than glorifying Christ, the pursuit of the church will be given to the method that is most effective in drawing people to church.

The problem is that secular people are not interested in worshiping and submitting to a holy God. Since carnal people are not attracted to a church full of holy people who worship a holy God, the church is tempted to secularize holiness to gain the attention and approval of a secular society. That is, to overcome the secular culture's natural disdain for holiness, the church is tempted to take that which is holy (the church of Jesus Christ) and *purposefully* cover it with secular wrapping paper to make it more attractive to secular people who are shaped by secular values.

For the sake of community outreach, the focus, energy, and resources of the church will begin to be turned away from doctrine, which leads to holiness, toward creating and maintaining various activities and programs that will lead to expansion. Success will be determined not on sinners being converted and the degree of holiness of the membership but on how effective the church is in reaching out to the community, as evidenced by its numerical growth.

Churches begin to compete to see who can acquire the most people. At this point, the race is on to see which church can build the most impressive facilities. Everything from coffee shops to fitness centers has been employed by churches to become more credible and attractive to people who judge churches based on worldly standards.

Today's churches not only seek to attract people by tangible means, such as programs, facilities, and coffee, but they utilize intangible means as well, such as creating the right ambiance. To reach society, churches seek to become culturally relevant by contextualizing their appearance, their worship, and their message to keep in touch with the secular culture. This may begin innocently enough by the church seeking to do away with unnecessary obstacles that may hinder the unchurched from stepping through the church doors. One of the first steps in creating an inviting atmosphere is downgrading the dress attire from shirt and tie to blue jeans and T-shirts.

This is not so much about the dress (that in and of itself is quite innocent) as it is creating a mood that feels less reverent and more casual. Then the church slowly moves away from congregational singing to a style of worship that seems more entertaining—like a concert performance. The more the senses can be stimulated through music and lighting, the better. These changes are important in creating a relevant atmosphere that non-Christians can enjoy and relate to—allowing a smooth and comfortable transition from a secular concert on Saturday night to worship on Sunday morning.

This shift in purpose has also affected the structure of church buildings. No longer do churches want to look "churchy," so they seek to do away with steeples and find an old warehouse or a concert hall to carry out its worship.

What's more, even how the church portrays Christ needs to be contextualized. The Lord Jesus no longer needs to be depicted as holy and with reverence but as one who is hip and relevant. Churches must work hard in staying *relevant* to the ever-changing trends and fashions of the world if they want to stay on the cutting edge. Those on the church staff (or at least those who are going to be seen on the stage) need to appear fashionable and attractive. The whole image or persona of the church needs to be eye-catching.

In the same way that a popular coffeehouse chain has successfully branded itself by creating a personal in-store experience for patrons, the church has sought to market itself by providing a similar multisensual impression for visitors. Traditional storefronts understand they need to offer more than a competitive price to compete with online retailers; they need to offer their customers an experience. If a potpourri of aromas, soft music mingling in the background, and relaxing earth-toned colors can stimulate coffee sales, maybe the right personalities, lighting, and music can stimulate church growth. In the end, to gain a broader hearing, the atmosphere, worship, message, and the image of the church need to be acceptable and attractive to the culture.

When Scripture speaks of man having a personal encounter with the Divine Presence, it depicts man as awestruck with the holiness of God and responding with fear, humility, and then joy. The atmosphere that was present when Isaiah entered the temple, with the cherubim covering their faces and crying, "Holy, Holy, Holy," prompting Isaiah to fall on his face and cry out, "Woe is me"

(Isa. 6:1–6), is not quite the mood the modern church is seeking to reproduce. Rather, a more relaxed and casual atmosphere, which resembling a football game, is the goal, where people cheer out a "J-E-S-U-S" chant before jamming out in their flip-flops. Again, these changes depict whom the church is seeking to please.

Minimizing the Unholiness of the World

After the *seeker-sensitive* church lowers the standard of holiness within the church, the next logical step is to raise the level of goodness of those outside the church. When it becomes hard to distinguish between the culture of the church and the culture of the world, the church will soon perceive mankind as being basically good. The great problem of society is not sin but hunger and other social issues. No longer does the world need Christ to be a Redeemer who saves mankind from its depravity but for Christ to be the great example who brings relief to the repressed, underprivileged, sick, and the hungry. The mission of the church shifts from redeeming sinners to redeeming the culture.

Churches that put man above God will, in the end, preach an anthropocentric, social gospel. These churches have abandoned the authoritative truth of God's Word, compromised holiness (e.g., condoning homo-sexuality), and have done away with the doctrine of depravity by exalting the goodness of mankind. In return, the best these liberal churches can do is help man help himself by providing some moral guidance and a few hot bowls of soup along the way.

A Warning from Charles H. Spurgeon

In 1888, Charles Spurgeon saw the church of his day compromise its purpose to broaden its influence in the world and issued this warning:

Men seem to say—It is of no use going on in the old way, fetching out one here and another there from the great mass. We want a quicker way. To wait till people are born again, and become followers of Christ, is a long process: let us abolish the separation between the regenerate and unregenerate. Come into the church, all of you, converted or unconverted. You have good wishes and good resolutions; that will do: don't trouble about more. It is true you do not believe the gospel, but neither do we. You believe something or other. Come along; if you do not believe anything, no matter; your "honest doubt" is better by far than faith. "But," say you, "nobody talks so." Possibly they do not use the same words, but this is the real meaning of the present-day religion; this is the drift of the times. I can justify the broadest statement I have made by the action or by the speech of certain ministers, who are treacherously betraying our holy religion under pretense of adapting it to this progressive age. The new plan is to assimilate the church to the world, and so include a larger area within its bounds. By semi-dramatic performances they make houses of prayer to approximate to the theatre; they turn their services into musical displays, and their sermons into political harangues or philosophical essays—in fact, they exchange the temple for the theatre, and turn the ministers of God into actors, whose business it is to amuse men. Is it not so, that the Lord's-day is becoming more and more a day of recreation or of idleness, and the Lord's house either a joss-house full of idols, or a political club, where there is more enthusiasm for a party than zeal for God? Ah me! the hedges are broken down, the walls are leveled, and to many there is, henceforth, no church except as a portion of the world, no God except as an unknowable force by which the laws of nature work.[1]

Please don't misunderstand. Community outreach, inviting non-believers to church, social activities, blue jeans, modernized

1   Charles H. Spurgeon, "No Compromise" in *Metropolitan Tabernacle Pulpit* (Pasadena, TX: Pilgrim, 1988), Vol. 34, No. 2047.

facilities, and cappuccinos are not wrong in and of themselves. A church should not be judged by if it has a steeple or not. Revising antiquated traditions and making changes to help welcome visitors can be a good thing. Helping those in need is worthy, and all churches should evangelize the lost. Moreover, what churchgoer would have a problem with a good cup of coffee?

The problem comes into play, however, when churches become more concerned about marketing and branding an image (by creating an aesthetic impression that appeals to the five senses) than they are about seeking to be known as the pillar and ground of the truth. The concern is when the church is more focused on creating an image based on outward aesthetics (i.e., buildings, style of music, choreographing, and staging the service) than building a reputation based on an inward beauty of holiness. When the church downplays its role as a means of sanctification for the saints and secularizes that which is meant to be holy to make the gospel more attractive to the world, they are in danger of losing track of their real purpose—God's glory.

The Church Should Not Mimic the World

John MacArthur reminds us that "worldliness is the sin of allowing one's appetites, ambitions, or conduct to be fashioned according to earthly values."[2] Therefore, when the church *knowingly* and *purposefully* runs after the trends and influences of the world to help gain the approval of the world, then the church itself becomes worldly.

What the world needs is not another worldly church. The church doesn't need to add Kool-Aid mix to the living waters to sweeten its appeal. Adding sweetener to the gospel not only dishonors Christ, it cannot satisfy those who are truly thirsty. The sick, the mournful, the dying, and those who know they are lost are not looking for

---

2   John MacArthur, *Ashamed of the Gospel* (Wheaton, IL: Crossway, 1993), xvii.

a cool Christianity or a message that has been contextualized to fit a Hollywood culture but a gospel that is serious, sincere, and unadorned. The old, plain gospel is still relevant to those who are perishing and still connects to those who are quickened by the Spirit to place their trust in Christ Jesus.

Inward Holiness Affects External Appearances

Flip-flops or suits is not the real issue, and legalism and asceticism are not the answer. Equating puritanical dress and traditional hymnology with holiness is not Scriptural, and trying to rid the church of all cultural influences is folly.

Legalism is not the answer to worldliness. Holiness does not originate from outside the person. Rather, holiness stems from within (Matt. 23:25–26). Churches that seek to establish holiness from the outside by imposing strict regulations will produce nothing but pride and self-righteousness within their membership. Enforcing outward laws can never change the heart. Instead, true holiness comes from above by means of the Spirit applying the truth of God's Word to the heart. This is why churches must seek to clean the inside of the cup before focusing on cleaning the outside of the cup (Matt. 23:26).

Churches that pride themselves in their strict dress code (or those that purposefully seek to look unfashionable and outdated) are in danger of doing the same thing as the churches that intentionally seek to brand themselves by being hip and trendy—both are placing their focus on the external. And when the focus is on the external, it shows whom the church is seeking to please—man.

Pursuing holiness is not so much about regulating the external (suits or flip-flops) as much as it is focusing on the inward devotion and love that the church has for God. Yet, private devotion to God will be reflected in one's external behavior and dress. Internal holiness of the heart does work itself out. When Christians are changed from within, others will notice by observing their conduct. As Christians become more concerned about the things of God, they will become less concerned about the things of the world (1 John 2:15–17). When Christian women desire to please God, they will naturally want to dress more modestly (1 Tim. 2:9). In other words, when holiness increases, worldliness decreases.

In this way, outward appearances do matter. For instance, Peter claims that the beauty which godly women should seek to put on display is not an outward beauty that consists of merely expensive and impressive clothing but an inward beauty that consists of gentleness and quietness of spirit (1 Peter 3:3–4). Paul even implies that immodesty and questionable apparel can distract others from seeing the inward beauty of the hidden person of the heart (1 Tim. 2:9–10). As Christian women decide how to dress, they need to check their motives and ask themselves whom they are seeking to please and to what they are seeking to draw others' attention—their outward or inward beauty?

Why would a local church desire to be known as "the church that is on the cutting edge"? This is placing the spotlight on the wrong thing. Rather, the reputation that every church should desire is one of unity, purity, and verity. It does not seem reasonable for a church seeking to promote the inward *beauty of holiness* within its membership to seek also an external image that corresponds with the vanity of the ever-changing customs of an increasingly secular culture. Just because we live in Vanity Fair does not mean we have to look like Vanity Fair to warn the lovers of Vanity Fair to forsake Vanity Fair.

Motives

Again, don't misunderstand! The answer is not for the church to shrink back from all cultural influences and do away with any concern for outward aesthetics. This is not only impossible, it's also not the real issue of concern. For instance, when Paul urged godly women to be more concerned about displaying their inward beauty than their external beauty, he was not suggesting that they cease combing their hair and eliminate all concern they may have for their outward looks. In the same way, there is a place for the beautification of church facilities, playing musical instruments with skill, and dressing appropriately for worship. Yet, these outward things are not to overshadow or distract others from what's important—the gospel of Jesus Christ.

Churches with different demographics will naturally look different. A megachurch in Seattle may not look like a small, rural church in Mississippi, but neither church should seek to brand itself by its external appearance. A cowboy church, a hipster church, a white-collar church, or blue-collar church may each be appealing to specific groups of people, but such branding places the focus on the wrong thing.

Thus, the real issue here is the *motive* behind such marketing and branding. What is the reason the church wants to appeal to people's physical senses? Are they seeking to honor Christ, or are they seeking to gain a broader hearing by appealing to people's desire to be entertained and have their physical senses stimulated by a multisensory experience? Why would a church *purposefully* seek to adorn the glorious gospel with images that are culturally known (even by lost people) to be edgy, risqué, and taboo? Churches also need to be careful that their motives are not driven by a hidden desire to shock conservatives, fundamentalists, and traditionalists by appealing to lost man's natural rebellious spirit.

Breaking through Cultural Barriers

Building a bridge and reaching out in love is needed. Yet the best way to break through cultural barriers and connect with sinners is by presenting a clear gospel spoken in love, sincerity, and humility. The biblical method of attracting sinners to Christ and to His church is not found in superficial marketing strategies but in the display of unity, purity, and verity. Those outside the church should see something in a church that they don't have, something that they envy, something that they need, and something that Hollywood cannot offer them—the holiness that only comes by the glorious gospel of Jesus Christ.

Truth and holiness are relevant to all people and transcend all cultural barriers. Man is universally seeking a remedy for his guilt, and thus, the gospel can connect with all types of sinners because it's the only real cure for a defiled conscience. This is good news for the church and the Christian. The church does not have to be a cowboy or hipster church to effectively reach, understand, and connect with cowboys or hipsters. The Christian must neither intentionally dress like a geek to witness to nerds nor get his or her body covered with ink to be an effective evangelist in the inner city. If you wear cowboy boots, fine, or if you wear flip-flops, fine; the important thing is not to seek unnecessary attention to your outward appearance and to make sure you carry the gospel to all people in love and humility. If people reject you, it will not be because they were offended by your outward appearance but because they were offended by your Master (John 15:20).

Conclusion

It's not necessary for the church to repackage the gospel in secular wrapping paper to make the altogether lovely One become more appealing and acceptable to the secular culture. The distinguishing mark of every true church should not be its facilities, its age-related programs, its style of music, or any other secondary issue. Instead, the distinguishing mark of every true church should be *the truth*.

Reaching the culture is a good objective, but it should not become the *main* objective. When it does, the church cannot reach the culture effectively. A compromised witness is the last thing the world needs. Rather the Scripture teaches that the objective of the church should be the pursuit of a holy God. The harder and faster the church runs after God (via the truth), the brighter its spiritual illumination will shine in this unholy and secular world. And only when the church is Christocentric and not ashamed of the whole counsel of God is it a true light in the world.

Review Questions

1. In what ways are local churches tempted to lose focus of their purpose in their attempt to reach the culture?

2. In what ways do you see local churches compromising their witness to broaden their appeal?

3. Why is it important for local churches to be God centered in their attempt to reach people?

4. Why is holiness more important than being appealing?

5. Why does holiness affect our outward actions?

6. Do appearances matter?

7. Why should the local church be God centered?

9

The Teaching
of the Church

MUCH OF CONTEMPORARY CHRISTIANITY has forsaken
its roots and has become overtly nonconfessional. Churches are
no longer Baptist, Presbyterian, or Methodist but have become
nondenominational. First Baptist Church has changed its name to
The Journey, and the Bible Church has become the New Life Church.
The Church on the Rock came out of the Assemblies of God, but
who is to know? For the sake of growth and inclusivity, churches
are afraid to define themselves and tell people what they believe.
Doctrinal ambiguity has replaced the old confessions of faith, and
contemporary Christianity seems quite content to identify itself
with only vague generalities. The goal is to *experience* Jesus and find
personal meaning and purpose without any clear definitions. This
new attitude is exemplified in this statement someone posted on
Facebook:

> Theology and doctrine are very rarely (if ever) a friend of
> Jesus. They are well-intentioned, but the enemy loves nothing
> more than to have God's children forego a vibrant, passionate

love relationship with Jesus and substitute it with doctrine and thesis statements. Please never open the Bible to find out what to tell others you believe; open God's Word to sit in His presence, talk with Him and have Him speak to you. Jesus hates to be researched. He is a person and invites you to know Him.

Though this sounds spiritual, it is naïve to think that it's possible to know Christ *experientially* without biblical doctrine. Such statements as this are not only naïve, they are contradictory. Those who make such claims are making a doctrinal statement and telling others what to believe.

This exchange of confessions for concessions is the new *mystical* theology of today's Christianity. There seem to be several reasons why contemporary Christianity has replaced their doctrinal confessions with vague and loose generalities: (1) indifference, (2) ignorance, (3) pragmatism, and (4) mysticism.

Of these four reasons, mysticism is the one we want to expose in this chapter. It is not that the other three reasons are irrelevant, but it appears that mysticism is the real root behind the other three. Before we jump into mysticism though, let us quickly highlight the first three reasons confessions have dropped from contemporary Christianity.

1. Indifference

Some Christians do not see any value in confessions of faith. It is not as if these believers are against confessions, they just haven't given them much thought. The thinking goes like this: doctrine is not all that important as long as people love Jesus. When looking for a new church to join, those in this group are not as concerned about the doctrinal standards of the church as much as with learning about the children's programs and musical style of worship. To them, what marks a good church is not its beliefs but its attractive programs.

2. Ignorance

Generally, this group consists of those who pride themselves in making the Bible their preferred confession of faith. "No creed but the Bible" is their creed. Those who pride themselves in this type of anti-creedal position generally think a creed or confession supplants the Word of God as the ultimate authority of faith and practice. This viewpoint may come from a well-intentioned heart, but it also stems from an uninformed mind. As B. H. Carroll explained, "There never was a man in the world without a creed. What is a creed? A Creed is what you believe. What is a confession? It is a declaration of what you believe. That declaration may be oral or it may be committed to writing, but the creed is there either expressed or implied."[1] Carroll's point is that it is impossible not to have a creed or confession. Just because a church refuses to adopt a confession or put their beliefs in writing does not mean that they are not creedal, in that they have their own interpretation of Scripture. To say, "I have no creed but the Bible," is like saying, "My only creed is my understanding of the Bible," yet refusing to elaborate on your understanding of the Bible. The fact that the church is commissioned to preach and teach the Bible is evidence that the church must make their interpretation of the Bible known to all.

3. Pragmatism

Another reason that churches do not want to define themselves doctrinally is that public confessions are thought to be too restrictive. Confessions get stored in the attic because the goal is to grow. Thus, the more inclusive the church is, the better. To accommodate today's objective, the church's creed is now "Open Minds, Open Hearts, and Open Doors." This creed is inclusive and shuts no religious person out. This type of ecumenical openness comes from a refusal to make a public stand for the truth.

1   B. H. Carroll, "Creeds and Confessions of Faith," in *Baptists and Their Doctrines*, eds. Timothy and Denise George (Nashville: Broadman & Holman, 1995), 81.

For a church to say they have an "open mind" is to say that they have not come to any conclusions as of yet. All visitors with their diverse opinions and diverse lifestyles are welcome to join in the ongoing discussion. To confirm and expose the depravity of man, for instance, may offend seekers and prevent them from coming to church and experiencing Jesus in worship. Thus, it is best to minimize doctrinal truth and keep love (a subjective emotion) and a wishy-washy Jesus as the focal point. These pragmatic ends, in their minds then, are the best way to grow the church and connect people with the love of Jesus.

Because doctrinal soundness is not a priority for the majority of churchgoing people, churches intentionally refuse to make doctrinal soundness their priority. Less truth means more people, sadly. And because their ultimate goal is to grow, those churches are content to confess as little as possible to remain within the bounds of Christian orthodoxy.

4. Mysticism

One of the main problems—if not the main problem—behind today's anti-confessional Christianity is mysticism. Mysticism is an attempt to find meaning without definitions. It seeks an existential experience for self-validation and a personal experience that "speaks to me" outside of Scripture. Because of a desire for something new or directly personal, seekers are not looking for doctrinal instruction.

For churches to help bring unbelieving seekers (who are not interested in knowing and obeying God) into a worshipful experience, they need to keep the focus off the truth of Scriptures— for unbelievers can enjoy worshiping as long as they don't know who and what they are worshiping. And if churches can keep the focus on the *emotions* of the worshiper, then unbelieving worshipers can worship without believing.

There need not be any doctrinal foundation behind the emotion provided the emotions are *authentic*. When words are used, it is not their objective meaning that is important but, rather, their subjective connotations. Vague religious terms such as *God*, *Spirit*, *Jesus*, and even the word *gospel* are fine as long as they are not clearly defined. It is better to allow worshipers to feel spiritual without having to think than to feel unspiritual because they were forced to think. If the words used in worship remain vague, worshipers can experience a transcendent moment without having to confront a holy God while they remain in their sins. And again, the more spiritual, transcendent, mystical, and vague the worship lyrics and the sermon are, the more likely it is to stimulate an emotional and ineffable experience for the worshiper.

The goal of these worshipers starts as a desire to have a spiritual connection with God, but the experience itself is sought out more than God Himself. "Here *I* am to worship," as the song goes, could lead to this type of self-focus. It is this drive and desire for a mystical experience today that acts as a thick, dark cloud seeping into the cracks of the contemporary church with the advertisement to bring about "authentic" worship. In short, for mysticism to work, clear doctrinal teaching must be left as a thing of the past.

The Nature of Mysticism

Mysticism may sound like a mysterious and difficult subject to get a handle on, but the basic tenets of mysticism are straightforward. In all the various forms of mysticism, there are three basic ideas:

1. Ultimate reality is ineffable or unknowable (transcending human language and rational thought).

2. The only way to know this ultimate reality is by some form of existential experience (by *existential* experience, I mean an experience that transcends the rational process of cognitive thought).

3. Once mystics or worshipers have experienced the ultimate
    reality, it is impossible for them to communicate or share
    this experience with others—for it remains ineffable and,
    thus, mysterious. Different types of mysticism have different
    labels for this "ultimate reality" and various methods of
    achieving this existential experience, but they all seek some
    form of connection with the ultimate reality that transcends
    the cognitive thought process.

The bottom line is that mysticism allows the worshiper or
religious seeker to have an experience without having to back it up
objectively with Scripture.

The Influence of Mysticism

The emergent church is nothing more than a form of mysticism—
an attempt to find meaning without absolutes. To think that the
rest of Christianity has remained uninfluenced by mysticism is
naïve. Churches across the globe have turned away from experience
rooted in doctrine toward experience rooted in mysticism.
Sermons have shifted away from theology (how to know and love
God) to motivational speeches (how to have your best life now).
When theological terms are used, they remain vague and subject
to diverse interpretations. Music has taken priority over preaching.
The rich and doctrinal lyrics of the old hymns that focus on the
work of Christ have been replaced with a few superficial, repetitious
words that focus on the emotions of the worshiper. Contemporary
worship is predominantly individuals marinating in their own
affections and love toward a vague God rather than the church
corporately praising the God of the Bible for His love as manifested
in the life, death, and resurrection of Jesus Christ.

The reason mysticism is so popular in churches is not necessarily
because it offers meaning and hope in a postmodern climate of
meaninglessness and despair but because it can make unspiritual
people feel spiritual. These mystical experiences are real for the
worshiper and easily created by the worship team. Dim the lights,

get people excited by the beat and rhythm of the music, throw in a few religious terms, turn the focus to the emotions of the worshiper, and—presto!—people feel spiritual.

Another reason mysticism is effective is that man is religious by nature and has an innate desire to worship. Create the right atmosphere, then give pagans an idol (or Americans a cool Jesus), and they will worship. To witness this superficial worship, all you have to do is follow your unconverted friends to church and watch them raise their hands as they lose themselves in the *act* of worship. This is not to say that the true Christian in the same pew is not worshiping the real Lord Jesus. But simply manipulating the atmosphere can create his neighbor's false worship. Hold back theology and give people emotionalism, and people will enjoy a mystical experience that feels spiritual.

The Correction for Mysticism

Of course, there are some parallels between mystical theology and biblical Christianity. A saving knowledge of the Lord Jesus Christ includes more than a cognitive understanding of the biblical truth declarations (James 2:19). By faith, people experience a personal knowledge of the Lord Jesus (Eph. 3:14–19). This saving knowledge brings about inexpressible love, joy, and peace. In addition, this experiential knowledge of Christ Jesus comes only by spiritual illumination. Thus, a personal knowledge of the Lord is incommunicable—for it's impossible to share our experiential knowledge of Christ Jesus with others.

With that said, biblical Christianity is not mysticism. The fundamental difference is that saving faith and an experiential knowledge of Christ Jesus do not come from an existential experience that transcends cognitive and rational thought. There is no leap of faith into the darkness but, rather, a leap of faith into the light of God's Word. Saving faith comes only by hearing, and hearing comes only by the articulated Word of God being clearly proclaimed (Rom. 10:17). To know Christ initially and to grow in the knowledge of the Lord requires knowledge of the Scriptures (John 17:17). Doctrine, even deep doctrine, is vital to the Christian life (2 Thess. 2:13). *Doctrine*, moreover, simply means biblical teaching. Therefore, if the church wants to help aid people in worship and spiritual growth, then they will place the focus on teaching God's written Word.

The error of mysticism is that it is founded on the false presupposition that God is ineffable and unknowable. Yes, we are bound by our finiteness, but this does not rule out the possibility of divine communication between God and man. First, man has been created in the image of God, which provides common ground between an infinite God and finite man. Because of this common ground, not only is man able to communicate with God, God is able to communicate with man. Second, God has communicated to man in natural and special revelation (Ps. 19:1–6).

Therefore, God is not unknowable. Furthermore, divine revelation is universally understandable, leaving all without excuse (Rom. 1:20).

What about the *noetic* effects of the fall—the results of depravity upon the mind? Does not Scripture say that the natural man is unable to discern spiritual truth (1 Cor. 2:14)? Yes, fallen man has been alienated from the life of God and has no personal knowledge of Him. Due to the depravity of his heart, man will remain incapable and unwilling to place his faith and confidence in God. But this does not mean that fallen man cannot rationally understand the truth-claims of Scripture. The Bible is neither irrational nor contrary to sense perception. In fact, the biblical worldview is the only worldview that makes sense of reality as perceived by the empirical senses. It is the only worldview rationally consistent with itself.

The problem with fallen man is not a lack of evidence or a want of understanding of the truth but an absence of appreciation and love for the truth. The light has come into the world, and the Bible says that man loved darkness rather than the light (John 3:19). The problem with man's thinking lies in his refusal to submit, not in lack of proof. Man loves himself. Man loves his perceived notion of autonomy. Man loves his sin. Therefore, man would rather believe a lie or accept an inconsistent worldview than submit to a holy God (2 Thess. 2:10–11). Man is bound to his depraved heart. This lack of submission is the problem, which is why the Lord said that even if a person were raised from the dead, it would not convince a sinner to repent (Luke 16:31).

The point is that divine revelation is effective in communicating truth to fallen man even if he does not accept it. Man's knowledge and rejection of the truth will be the very thing that condemns him on the day of judgment.

A Case for Confessions

The remedy for mysticism is not to eliminate emotions and experiences from the Christian faith. This would lead to dead orthodoxy indeed. Emotions are vital to the Christian faith, and there is no salvation without an experiential knowledge of Christ. Praise songs have their place to express the emotions of the worshiper.

Even so, the answer to mysticism is to ensure that our experiences and emotions are rooted in biblical truth. This is because God has chosen to change the heart by the truth. There is no personal encounter with God apart from the truth.

Again, my primary concern here is to call attention to the popular *self-focused* mysticism of our day. There is a place needed, however, in all our walks for a Spirit-led, mystical experience of truth and of Christ that flows in harmony with Scripture but never outside of or in contradiction to it. The response of our hearts and thoughts in a true type of biblical mysticism always exalts Christ and not the experience itself.

Conclusion

Even though everything in the universe is in flux, God is constant, for the great I Am never changes. God is the ultimate reference point, and the absolute and unchanging God has broken through the transcendent wall that separates the infinite from the finite and has clearly spoken to us in His Word—the foundation of our faith. Being made in the likeness of God, we are proper recipients of this communication. Yet, because of the fall, we can misread it as well. Because the Bible can be both understood and misunderstood, truth is not relative. Rather, truth and error are antithetical; an interpretation of Scripture is either right or wrong. Either people understand the intended meaning of Scripture correctly, or they don't.

Because truth is knowable and absolute, confessions of faith are all the more important. If it were impossible to understand the Bible, or if it were impossible to misunderstand, then no confession of faith would be needed. But seeing that there are both correct and incorrect interpretations, it is essential to know what a church believes to compare their confession with the Word of God. Every church member or potential church member has the right to know how the church interprets the Scripture. It is not enough, with all the false teaching floating around, for churches just to say they believe the Bible or simply love Jesus. That kind of generic confession says little. It is the truth that saves, and it is the truth that sanctifies. It is time for the local church to stop hiding behind vague generalities and undefined religious terms for the sake of unfounded mystical experiences and time to start clearly stating what we believe.

Review Questions

1. What are the four reasons noted in this chapter on why churches minimize doctrine?

2. Why is pragmatism such a problem in churches?

3. Why is it impossible for believers and churches not to have a profession of faith?

4. What is mysticism?

5. Why is mysticism a threat to sound doctrine?

6. Why is mysticism so appealing?

7. Why should churches confess what they believe?

8. Why are confessional statements important?

Part 4

The Worship of the Church

God is spirit, and those who worship him
must worship in spirit and truth.

— John 4:24

10

The Theology of Worship

GIVEN THAT THE PURPOSE of the church is to promote maturity by unity, purity, and verity, then the specific activities and functions of the church should be focused on achieving these broader objectives. Many churches, however, have gone astray here. The emphasis has been taken off these biblical objectives and has been placed on secondary or, worse, man-centered concerns. Numerical growth has too often become of first importance so that whatever it takes to fill the pews is often employed without any consideration of its scriptural basis. In so doing, many churches have abandoned the biblical blueprint, and in its place have become pragmatic, relativistic, commercial, and consumer driven.

This type of the-end-justifies-the-means philosophy reduces the church to nothing more than a powerless business. Inordinate, age-related activities that disconnect the family and create "your own personal dynamic worship experience" must be delivered as advertised. Why has this bait-and-switch model become so popular? Simply because this is what modern churchgoers are looking for in an already-crammed lifestyle. Regretfully, many people choose a church not because of its faithfulness to Scripture and unity and Christlikeness of its members (no matter the size) but for the musical style of worship and the number of programs and social activities offered. People seek social connections, and thus, they are attracted to the churches with the most people. The parents give up their choice to choose a church under the guise of wanting what is best for the children. And so goes the market of a buffet of church choices and a rush to offer the next tantalizing technique. Such seeker-sensitive churches have resorted to giving people what they want, not what they need. They have switched from trying to please God to the snare of pleasing men. Since such churches run more like a business, they are ready to supply whatever becomes in demand.

The early church had a much simpler approach by focusing on the preached Word, fellowship, and prayer (Acts 2:42). As undramatic as it may sound to modern ears, this is what the early church sought to do. Replacing these biblical pursuits with secondary or man-centered interests can only result in a nominal Christianity.

To understand why the church should worship God through the prescribed means, it is important to understand how worship works. Ultimately, what determines how a church attempts to worship God is the church's theology.

In other words, although the cultural and demographic makeup of a congregation can influence its worship, the main feature that shapes worship is the church's theology. Every church has core beliefs about God, salvation, and man. Even bad and poor theology is still theology, and every church's theology shapes its worship. Roman Catholic worship centers around the Mass because Catholic theology of salvation is based on the sacraments. The theology of Charles Finney led many in the church to shift from a Word-oriented worship to an emotionally driven service. Why?

Because, according to Finney, salvation was the result of emotional appeal and persuasion. Likewise, pragmatism is the theology that ultimately drives the seeker-sensitive church. Thus, the demands of the consumer have caused the church to turn its worship into a form of entertainment with a therapeutic, motivating lesson. *Creativity* in worship, which is emphasized by the emergent church, is based on an ever-changing theology that contains no absolutes.

The takeaway here is that theology matters when it comes to worship. We learn what a church believes about God, man, and salvation by the way the church worships God. For this reason, the church needs to worship in a manner that reflects a sound theology of worship. If the church desires to worship God, it is fundamental that the church first knows what *biblical* worship is.

Worship Is *from* God

Worship is rendering to God the glory (value), honor, and praise due His name. Yet such worship is impossible from an unbelieving heart and an unilluminated mind. Before anyone can properly worship God, they must know God.

Therefore, man will never worship God acceptably apart from Divine revelation. This is because worship is the result of God first revealing Himself to man. Only after man sees who God truly is and is given a heart to fear, love, and appreciate Him will he truly submit and dedicate his life and praise to God. This God-initiated worship means that where there is no revelation and knowledge of God, there is no true worship of God (John 4:22). For without sound theology, worship is idolatry.

Conversely, the more we know about God, the deeper our worship of God will be. In the end, God must first reveal Himself before man will *truly* worship God. Therefore, worship is always a response to the truth that God has revealed about Himself in His Word.

Worship Is *through* Christ

Worship is from God, and God has chosen to reveal Himself through Christ alone. Our knowledge of God comes to us through the person of His Son—Jesus Christ (2 Cor. 4:4). Furthermore, because of man's impurity and unworthiness, worship must always travel back to God through Christ (1 Tim. 2:5). There is no other way to the Father except through the atoning work of the Lord Jesus Christ.

Worship Is *in* the Truth

Christ Jesus will never be made known to us except through the truth that is found in Holy Scripture (Rom. 10:14–15). If worship is the by-product of the knowledge of God, then worship must be rooted in the truth of Scripture. Faith is at the very heart of worship, and worshipers must live by every inspired word that has come from the mouth of God—words that are recorded in Holy Scripture. Again, worship without theology is idolatry.

Worship Is *by* the Spirit

We must worship in truth, but the truth will never penetrate the heart apart from the illumination of the Holy Spirit (1 Cor. 2:10–16). Accordingly, we must also worship in the Spirit. Yet, the Spirit speaks to us by, in, and through the Scriptures. If the church today yearns to hear the voice of the Spirit, then the church must teach the Scriptures. Worship in the Spirit, then, must be based on the truth of Scripture. This is why the Spirit must empower our worship if worship is to be acceptable to God.

Worship Is *with* Holiness

Spirit-illuminated truth sanctifies and changes the heart of the worshiper (John 17:17). Fear, love, adoration, and praise can only come from a heart that has been purified by God's Word. Worship happens when the mind and heart of the worshiper is changed from rebellion and pride to submission and humility. However, humility and devotion come only from the heart being spiritually renewed and changed by the empowered truth of God's Word. It is only when the worshiper has been sanctified by the Word that the worshiper can offer acceptable worship to God. Without *holiness*, worship is in vain.

Worship Is *to* God

Only after worshipers have been changed will they naturally, freely, and willingly offer up their reverence, submission, praise, and servitude to God (Matt. 16:17). Only after they have been given new eyes to see the majesty of God will they see that He alone is worthy of all their praise. Worship comes from God; it is to go back to God, for to God alone belongs the glory.

Conclusion

In short, God is the author, enabler, and object of our worship. We cannot worship God without the power of God. The Spirit of God must illuminate the truth of the Son of God so we can give glory to God. We cannot worship God without worshiping in the Spirit and without worshiping in the truth. If this is the theology of worship, how worship works, then it is impossible to worship God apart from the Word of God.

Review Questions

1. How do we learn about what a church believes by watching how the church worships?

2. Can we initiate true worship? Why or why not?

3. Why is true worship from God?

4. Why does acceptable worship have to be mediated through Christ?

5. What did Christ mean when He stated that we must worship in truth?

6. How does the Spirit enable worship?

7. Can we worship God without holiness?

11

The Elements
of Worship

BECAUSE TRUE WORSHIP IS the proper response to the Word of God, we cannot worship God apart from the Word of God. And, if we cannot worship God apart from His Word, then we are not free to invent new approaches to worshiping God just because they help facilitate an emotional experience. We cannot truly experience what we do not know, and we cannot know God unless He reveals Himself to us in His Word. Adoration, godly fear, obedience, and praise come only from a heart that has been illuminated by God's Word. Therefore, God's Word must be central to the life and worship of the church. In other words, where the Word is absent, there is neither a true church nor true worship.

For this reason, worship is restricted to the divine means by which God has promised to communicate His Word to us. These means, known as the *ordinary means of grace*, include preaching God's Word, reading God's Word, singing God's Word, praying God's Word, seeing God's Word in the ordinances, and fellowshipping around God's Word. And the one thing the ordinary means of grace all have in common is that they are all the prescribed means God has given the church to communicate His Word.

What, then, are the true biblical activities of the local church? According to the Scriptures, the church is to come together to glorify Christ in pursuing unity, purity, and verity by focusing on five simple activities.

1. Worship God through Preaching the Word

Martyn Lloyd-Jones believed that preaching is not only the principal task of the church but that everything else performed by the church is subsidiary to it.[1] And John Calvin said: "The church is built up solely by outward preaching, and that the saints are held together by one bound only."[2]

Some churches, however, are under the impression that singing (because of the power that music has on our emotions) is the most effective means of worshiping God. Consequently, the time allotted for singing has increased, while sermons have become shorter. Forty years ago, Martyn Lloyd-Jones noted the church's shift away from preaching:

> It has been illuminating to observe these things; as preaching has declined, these other things have been emphasised; and it has been done quite deliberately. It is a part of this reaction against preaching; and people have felt that it is more dignified to pay this greater attention to ceremonial, and form, and ritual. Still worse has been the increase in the element of entertainment in public worship—the use of films and the introduction of more and more singing; the reading of the Word and prayer shortened drastically, but more and more time given to singing.[3]

---

1 See Martyn Lloyd-Jones, *Preaching and Preachers* (Grand Rapids: Zondervan, 1972), 26.

2 John Calvin, *Institutes of the Christian Religion*, ed. John T. McNeill, trans. Ford Lewis Battles (Philadelphia, PA: Westminster Press, 1977), 4.1.5.

3 Lloyd-Jones, *Preaching and Preachers*, 16–17.

It is true that congregational singing is an essential part of worship, but it should not be the principal part of the service. Look at how many times in the New Testament the words *preach*, *preaching*, *teach*, and *teaching* are recorded in comparison to *sing*, *singing*, *hymns*, *songs*, and other related words. Preaching is the predominant activity that Christ, His apostles, and the early church carried out throughout the New Testament. If churches want to get back to the biblical blueprint of how to worship God, then preaching must be placed back in its biblical priority!

Why is it that churches have taken their attention off preaching and placed it on singing? Often it is because singing is entertaining and more appealing to the unchurched. If not for this reason, it may be that music can create such a powerful worship experience for the worshiper. Emotion is often elevated above knowledge. Conversely, biblical and doctrinal preaching is viewed as boring and dull, even convicting and hard to endure, by many.

Singing, on the other hand, is enjoyable and even exciting. Music has the power to create a mystical experience of worship, even for unbelievers. It is here that the unconverted can feel at ease and somewhat spiritual. The more dynamic the music and the more that positive feelings can be aroused, the better. Through choreographing the music, even unbelievers can enjoy a dynamic worship experience. This approach does a better job of filling the pews, so why not switch?

In following the outline of the Scriptures, however, God is most glorified and the saints are most edified by the Word of God being accurately explained to the mind and properly applied to the heart by the power of the Holy Spirit, not by an arousing of the emotions through the power of music. Preaching that both opens the mind to sound doctrine and cuts to the heart with practical application is what is needed. Preaching exhibits God's glory and is the primary means by which He has chosen to save the lost and sanctify the saints (1 Cor. 1:18; Eph. 4:11–15). Deep preaching will result in deep worship.

2. Worship God through Praying the Word

A second vital activity of the church is individual and corporate prayer. The reality and vitality of a church is its prayer life (Matt. 21:13). Where there is a church with little to no prayer, there is a church with little to no life.

Prayerlessness is why churches can become so weak; prayerlessness is why there can be so little efficacy in the preaching time slot. And it is for lack of corporate (and private) prayer that people can become so dull of hearing in today's contemporary church. Prayer is like the extension cord that plugs into heaven; without it, there is simply no power. The church pews may be full on Sunday morning, but look at how empty they are come prayer meeting on Wednesday night.

If the church were truly dependent on God, then it would cease taking surveys and consulting marketing firms and fall before God in private and corporate prayer (Ps. 127:1). Oh, if churches could just get a hold of the magnitude of prayer—for it is not only a good activity, it is *essential*.

3. Worship God through Seeing the Word in the Ordinances

The church has been entrusted with two biblical ordinances: believer's baptism and the Lord's Supper (1 Cor. 11:26, Acts 2:41). Baptism is a public testimony of repentance of sin and an act of obedience to the Lord. Although baptism is not essential to salvation, it is highly unlikely that a person has been truly born again without an eager desire to follow the Lord in this first command that God gives the new Christian (Acts 2:38). Baptism is a public confession of Christ (Matt. 10:32–33) that evidences to the church and the world that there has been a radical transformation within. Baptism is also a visible sermon. It demonstrates a spiritual reality of one's death to sin and resurrection to the newness of life in Christ Jesus.

The Lord's Supper is a memorial of Christ's death (1 Cor. 11:26). As with baptism, the Lord's Supper is a visible sermon that illustrates a spiritual reality. More than that, the Lord's Supper not only depicts Christ's death but it also shows the spiritual communion between Christ and His people. It is called *Communion* because it shows how Christ and His people are united in one body (1 Cor. 10:16). The partaking of the bread and the wine illustrates how God's people have union and fellowship with Christ by faith. The partaking of the elements collectively by God's people pictures how they are equally united as well.

4. Worship God through Singing the Word

Worshiping the Lord in song is a Spirit-engendered desire for Christians. Although it was pointed out that the preached Word should be the focal point of the worship service, corporate singing of the praises of God should not be minimized. The Bible instructs the church to address, teach, and admonish one another through psalms, hymns, and spiritual songs (Eph. 5:19; Col. 3:16). Singing is a wonderful means of expressing one's deepest feelings of joy, admiration, and praise toward Christ. Therefore, a healthy worship service includes heartfelt, fervent, Spirit-led songs rooted in the glorious truths of God's Word.

Once again, if the objective of the church is to glorify Christ in the promotion of spiritual unity, purity, and verity, then our worship in song needs to reflect that objective. Regardless of what musical style is utilized in the service, these are the questions that need to be answered:

1. Are the lyrics of our songs doctrinally sound and Christ centered?

2. Does the musical style promote corporate participation among the brethren?

3. Is the manner or mode in which we worship reverent and holy?

Although a contemporary expression of worship can be spiritually refreshing, worship that is directed to a holy God should never be driven by our secular culture (Lev. 10:3). We must remember that secularism is the very opposite of holiness. Worship should never be casual. In Scripture, some died for not taking worship more seriously (see Lev. 10:1–2; 1 Cor. 11:30).

5. Worship God through Fellowship around the Word

Another one of the major activities of the early church is Christian fellowship (Acts 2:42). With community and unity as biblical objectives of the church, fellowship will find its place.

Biblical fellowship is the Holy Spirit ministering to the saints through the spiritual interaction of believers with each other. It is the Spirit ministering to one believer by means of another believer. The Holy Spirit lives within all believers, and it is the Holy Spirit within believers that makes Christian fellowship sanctifying. The love that Christians have for God and for one another, manifested in their fellowship and spiritual conversation, is edifying to the saints. The gathering and fellowshipping of the saints is a biblical means of spiritual growth. In this way, spiritual fellowship is a means of grace, and the local church should not neglect it.

Christian fellowship, nevertheless, seems to have lost its importance in the priorities of many church members—five minutes before and five minutes after the Sunday morning service seems to suffice today's churchgoers. Spiritual fellowship around Christ, however, is not something that can be neglected by either Christians or churches striving after the New Testament model.

True Christians love one another. They love the Lord and thus desire to be around those who have the Lord living in their hearts. Christians need the Lord, and because Christians have the Lord within, they need each other. Because of this internal reality, churches need to provide the opportunity for Christians to be around one another externally.

Practically, churches must be deliberate in making adequate time for fellowship for members to have the opportunity to carry out their responsibilities toward one another. If church members are required by the Scriptures to be dedicated to one another, love one another, and so forth, they cannot perform these responsibilities apart from spending sufficient time together, both on Sundays and on other days of the week.

Therefore, a mark of a healthy church is not only a praying church but also a church that regularly provides and encourages sufficient time for spiritual fellowship.

Conclusion

Although there will be other activities within church life, preaching, praying, singing, and participating in the ordinances are the elements of worship that drive them all. These are the activities God prescribed to the church as a means of communicating and applying the written Word of God. It is only when these means of grace are faithfully carried out that the church should expect the Spirit's presence.

Review Questions

1. What are the prescribed activities or means given to the church to worship God?

2. What do all these activities have in common?

3. Why is it impossible to worship God without the communication of God's Word?

4. Is the church free to worship God anyway it wants?

5. Why is preaching a principal means of worship?

6. Why does shallow doctrine lead to shallow worship?

7. Why is fellowship a part of the activities of the church?

8. Does the Spirit work without the truth? Explain.

12

The Principles
of Worship

"IT DOESN'T MATTER HOW WE WORSHIP," some may think, "as long as we are worshiping God." Sadly, this is what many worshipers believe, and it is why almost anything is permissible in worship services nowadays.

Yet when we read the Scriptures, we learn that God has killed worshipers not because they worshiped a false god but because they did not worship the true God in the manner in which God has prescribed (Lev. 10; 1 Cor. 11:30). God is not simply concerned that we worship Him; He is also concerned about *how* we worship Him.

Based on the theology of worship, explained in the previous chapter, there are at least seven biblical principles that regulate our worship, principles that transcend cultural influences.

1. Worship Must Be God Centered

To what degree should worship be directed toward and pleasing to God, and to what degree should worship be enjoyable for the church and sensitive to the seeker?

According to Scripture, worship is not 50/50 or even 90/10 but 100 percent theocentric (God centered). Not only is worship to be directed entirely toward God, but it will also only edify the saints and convict the lost to the degree that it glorifies God. Man-centered worship neither matures the body of Christ nor convicts sinners of their innate unworthiness to be in the presence of God.

2. Worship Must Be Word Centered

To what degree should worship be Word driven, and to what degree should worship be Spirit led? In other words, how much should worship be objective and directed toward the mind, and how much of worship should be subjectively felt and expressed from the heart? To what degree should the worship leader or praise team seek to arouse the emotions of the congregation by the tempo and style of music?

According to Scripture, the church is to worship in spirit and truth (John 4:24). No doubt, worship needs to be objectively based on the truth and subjectively felt and expressed within the heart. Even so, the church is called to fix its worship on the objectivity of the fixed Word of God and not on the subjective feelings and various spiritual experiences.

A. Worship must be regulated by the Word because the Spirit convicts, comforts, empowers, and sanctifies the saints through the Word. That is, the Spirit works in and by the Word, and the subjective feelings must flow from the objective truth of God's Word (Heb. 4:12). The Word is the sword of the Spirit that cuts to the heart (Eph. 6:17). That is to say, the Spirit has chosen to use the Scriptures (that He has inspired) to inflame faith, love, and devotion to God.

B. Worship must be regulated by the Word because the church does not have the authority or the ability to impart the Holy Spirit (John 3:8). Therefore, the church must focus on what it has been given the responsibility to do: sing, preach, and observe the ordinances. Spirit-empowered worship comes not by manipulating or even choreographing the emotional atmosphere but by hearing the Word of God being preached and sung.

C. Worship must be regulated by the Word because it is the Word that the Spirit has given us to test and examine various spiritual and subjective experiences (1 John 4:1).

D. Worship must be regulated by the Word because our emotions will lead us astray if not rooted and flowing out of the objective truth of God's Word.

E. Worship must be regulated by the Word because there is no spiritual edification without the cognitive understanding of the truth. The necessity for the interpretation of tongues was because rare emotionalism experienced by individuals was of no spiritual value in congregational worship. Spiritual edification requires an understanding of the mind. If we sing with our spirits, as Paul says, let us sing with our minds also; when it comes to worship, the engagement of the mind is vital (1 Cor. 14:15–16).

Godly emotions (e.g., love, praise, adoration) are a response to Word-centered worship. For these reasons, worship must be Word centered.

3. Worship Must Be Holy

How much should worship be sacred and expressed in holiness, and how much should worship be contextually influenced and aimed at reaching the secular culture?

While it is impossible to remove all cultural influences from worship, the church should never purposefully shape its worship to resemble customs of secular culture (especially the unholy culture of pop America). Worship to a holy God by a holy people should always be holy in its nature, practice, expression, and outward form.

Worship Is Holy by Its Very Nature

Worship is a sacred and holy act empowered by the Holy Spirit and directed toward a holy God. That is, looking back at the theology of worship, we learn that worship comes from a heart that has been sanctified by the truth. Worship takes place when God meets His people in their cultural context then sanctifies them by the truth so that they may move into the presence of God, who dwells in heavenly places.

Worship, in other words, is leaving the courtyard of this world through the veil of Christ Jesus into the holy of holies. Therefore, as worshipers ascend the steps to the throne of God, the cares of this world should be left behind.

Worship Must Be Holy in Practice

God does not receive the praises of men when they harbor sin in their hearts (Ps. 66:18). Those who seek to worship God must first acknowledge, confess, and repent of their sins before they can lift their praises to a holy God in an acceptable way (Matt. 5:24).

Worship Must Be Holy in Expression

It is a fearful thing to enter into the presence of a holy God (Ps. 5:7). Worship is never a casual affair, for we are not entering into the presence of a mere man but a transcendent and holy God. Let "us offer to God acceptable worship, with reverence and awe" (Heb. 12:28). We are to rejoice, but we are to "rejoice with trembling" (Ps. 2:11). Therefore, to view and behave as if Christ Jesus is our "homeboy" is to treat the Holy One of Israel with contempt.

Worship Must Be Holy in Outward Form

Some have died (both in the Old and New Testaments) because they did not approach God in a holy and acceptable fashion. The church is called to worship in the beauty of holiness (Ps. 29:2; 96:9). If the outward form of worship did not matter, why did God tell Moses to take off his shoes when he came close to the burning bush?

It is a false premise to think that worship needs to be culturally contextualized to be more effective in reaching the culture. This is because what is meant by contextualization is not making the gospel plain and easy to understand but making the gospel more appealing and attractive to society by integrating secular-sounding music, a hip and cool Jesus, and trendy fashions into worship. The more secular the worship, the more society will worship, or so goes the logic.

The problem, however, is that true worship will never be enjoyable to a secular culture. Unbelievers cannot and do not worship God. Churches can aid the unconverted in enjoying a mystical style of worship that appeals to the senses, but they can never cause them to enjoy and delight themselves in the holiness of God.

If anything, the world should feel uncomfortable and convicted in the presence of God. Holiness in worship doesn't need to equal the outdated and puritanical customs of the past, but holiness also does not include the desire to mimic the pop culture of Hollywood and MTV—a culture that is so overtly associated with rebellion and ungodliness.

Those who want to know where the dividing line is (the line that separates holiness from worldliness) are those who want to see how close they can come to that edge. Instead, the church should desire to be pure in every detail of its worship—everything questionable, offensive, risqué, edgy, or even a little shady should be avoided (1 Thess. 5:22). Let us dwell on the words of Richard Baxter, who reminded us:

> Remember the perfections of that God whom you worship, that he is a Spirit, and therefore to be worshipped in spirit and truth; and that he is most great and terrible, and therefore to be worshipped with seriousness and reverence, and not to be

dallied with, or served with toys or lifeless lip-service; and that he is most holy, pure, and jealous, and therefore to be purely worshipped; and that he is still present with you, and all things are naked and open to him with whom we have to do.[1]

May the Lord help the church from being conformed to the world, and may God's people forever seek to worship God in purity, by the power of the Spirit and the enlightenment of His Word.

4. Worship Must Not Focus on the Physical

What is the proper use of tangible objects within spiritual worship?

Physical objects and outward rituals were all a vital part of old-covenant worship. Locality, the use of animal sacrifices, the temple, temple furnishings, priestly garments, incense, and various other corporeal objects were utilized in worship. In fact, old-covenant worship was not acceptable apart from the use of these physical objects.

Today, Roman Catholic worship is closely tied to the physical. To facilitate worship, the Catholic Church has constructed massive cathedrals, implemented the use of icons, erected statues and altars, and adorned their ministers with priestly garb. All these objects help create a visible and tangible dimension to worship. To engage the other empirical senses (e.g., smell, hearing) the Catholic Church has implemented the use of incense, which stimulates an aromatic sensation, and various sounds that subjectively point to the transcendent God.

Protestant contemporary worship, similarly, has moved to a multisensory expression of worship. Dim lighting, candles, incense, loud energetic music, video, and other visual effects are there to assist the flesh in having an emotional experience. All these things create quite a sensation for the worshiper.

1   Richard Baxter, "A Christian Directory," in *The Practical Works of Richard Baxter* (London: George Virtue, 1838), 1:179.

True worship, on the other hand, cannot be manufactured through the stimulation of the physical senses but by the truth being spiritually illuminated to the heart of faith. Why must worship be spiritual rather than physical, it may be asked? The rejoinder is simple: "God is spirit, and those who worship him must worship in spirit and truth" (John 4:24). Worshipers cannot see the kingdom of God and the invisible Christ unless they are born again and given the eyes of faith (John 3:5–8; Heb. 11:1). The natural man, therefore, cannot worship God, whom he cannot see.

Those who are unable to discern spiritual truth must turn worship into a fleshly experience. Those who do not appreciate sound doctrine must look to merely an emotional experience. Those in the flesh must worship in the flesh through the stimulation of the physical senses by that which is tangible and visible. John Owen put it this way: "To the natural man, therefore, no religious worship is pleasing unless he can see something of glory and splendor. But no one sees the glory of spiritual worship unless he himself is also spiritual."[2] Martyn Lloyd-Jones gave this analysis: "The greater the amount of attention that has been paid to this aspect of worship—namely the type of building, and the ceremonial, and the singing, and the music—the less spirituality you are likely to have."[3]

No doubt, true worship will take place within buildings and with the use of various corporeal objects, such as songbooks, pulpits, and even the Bible itself. The ordinances also bring physical elements into congregational worship—water, bread, and wine. Yet faith (that is at the heart of worship) attaches itself not to the physical but to the spiritual and to the truth. Music and buildings may help facilitate worship, but unless worship is carried out in spirit and truth, it becomes nothing more than an emotional experience produced by stimulation of the physical senses.

2　John Owen, *Biblical Theology,* trans. Stephen P. Westcott (Morgan, PA: Soli Deo Gloria, 2002), 665.

3　Martyn Lloyd-Jones, *Preaching and Preachers* (Grand Rapids: Zondervan, 1972), 267.

5. Worship Must Be Orderly

How much of worship should be orderly, and how much of worship should be free and spontaneous?

According to 1 Corinthians 14:26–33, a worship service is not a free-for-all where individual Christians can do as they will. There are proper times when individuals can share a word or give a testimony in the service. However, even under the influence of the Spirit, Christians are called by God to submit to the proper order of the service (1 Cor. 14:32). This is because the goal of corporate worship is for collective edification of the whole congregation, not for individual expression of praise. Anything that draws unnecessary attention to self or causes others to be distracted should be rejected. Although Scripture does not lay out an explicit order of worship, it does make it clear that everything must be done decently and orderly (1 Cor. 14:40).

6. Worship Must Be Congregation Centered

How much of worship should be driven by musical arrangements, instruments, and lead vocalists, and how much of worship should be driven by congregational singing? And which is better, singing contemporary Christian music or the old hymns of the faith?

All things being equal, a song written five hundred years ago or a song written yesterday makes little to no difference. It is wonderful to sing hymns that have been sung by multiple generations of Christians. This shows doctrinal continuity and ecumenical unity within the historical church. Songs that have stood the test of time should not be disregarded. Conversely, singing new songs is also encouraging for the church. The gift of writing biblical and spiritual songs did not end with Isaac Watts and John Newton. Thankfully, many contemporary Christian songs will be sung for many generations to come.

The real issue is not between traditional or contemporary music as much as it is the priority between worship bands and congregational singing. Which should be most prominent: the music, the instruments, the lead vocalist(s), or the human voices of the assembly of the saints? Is our attention constantly being drawn to what is taking place on the stage, or is our worship principally assisted by the voices surrounding us in the pews?

According to the Scriptures, the reason singing is a vital part of corporate worship isn't because of the power that music has in stimulating our emotions. We sing corporately because of the mutual edification received by the saints joyfully singing biblical lyrics to one another (Eph. 5:19). Let every musical instrument praise the Lord, but it is the human voice that is best suited to lift up praises to God. As spiritual fellowship is spiritually beneficial, hearing our brothers and sisters sing unto the Lord is a spiritual means of instruction and encouragement (Col. 3:16). We are aided in our love for God when we hear our brothers and sisters expressing their love for God.

We cease to contribute to congregational worship when we lose ourselves in personal worship and forget our responsibilities toward our brothers and sisters around us. The benefit of corporate worship is found in the collective voices of the assembly harmonizing together as one body. God is more glorified when the saints worship together in one spirit and one mind than when individuals worship independently. Benjamin Keach, who was instrumental in reintroducing singing into corporate worship, said:

> Know my brethren, 'that God loves the gates of Zion more than all the dwelling places of Jacob' (Ps. 87:2). Therefore, the public worship of God ought to be preferred before private. (1.) This supposes there must be a visible church. (2.) And that they frequently meet together to worship God.[4]

---

4 Benjamin Keach, *The Glory of a True Church* (Conway, AR: Free Grace Press, 2015), 77.

It is not so much about traditional or contemporary worship as much as which style of music best facilitates congregational worship. Any music that hinders congregational participation and takes the focus away from the voices of the collective assembly is unbiblical. A church can worship without a band, but it cannot worship without the voices of the congregation singing. For this reason, the musicians and lead vocalists are to assist congregational involvement. They are there to aid, not dominate. They are not to draw attention to themselves. They are to remind themselves constantly that their primary goal is not to be artistically creative by displaying their gifts but to aid the congregation in collectively praising God and edifying each other with their voices. As John the Baptist sought to decrease so that Christ might increase, those facilitating the musical side of worship should seek to hide behind the voices of the saints. Only when the musicians and lead vocalists are supporting the singing of the congregation are they properly assisting the church in worshiping God.

When worship is congregation centered, the musical arrangement, lighting, volume of microphones, and instruments are to be deliberately monitored to assist rather than override corporate worship. Gifted musicians often prefer complex arrangements, but typically, congregations sing louder when the songs are familiar and predictable. Moreover, if congregational singing is a biblical priority, then every church member has a responsibility to minister to each other through the instrument of their voice. Singing songs, hymns, and spiritual songs to one another is a biblical command.

7. Worship Must Follow the Regulative Principle of Worship

What are the scriptural means of worship, and how much freedom does the church have in introducing new modes of worship within the church service?

There are certain prescribed means of worship—prayer, preaching and teaching, public reading of the Word, singing (psalms, hymns, and spiritual songs), and observing the ordinances (baptism and the Lord's Supper). Many have added to this list (e.g., burning incense, drama, dancing, video). Some are under the persuasion that these additional elements can be even more effective in facilitating worship. Yet the church does not have the freedom to introduce new forms of worship within the service (Lev. 10:1–3). Neither are prayer, preaching, singing, and the ordinances something that the church has the liberty to remove.

"What's the big deal?" someone may ask. Well, these latter elements alone are the ordained activities given to the church as the means of grace. By *the means of grace,* it is meant that they are the modes of worship God has promised to bless and to use to build up the body of Christ and the divine methods God has chosen to communicate truth to His people. However, incense, drama, or additional activities (no matter how exciting they may be) have no such promise attached to them.

In addition, the church has no authority to bind the conscience of the saints with non-Scriptural practices. Much like the church does not have the biblical authority to enforce homeschooling upon the congregation, the church does not have the right to subject God's people to additional activities within the service. Rather than seeking to add to the service new modes of worship, let the church seek to do that which has been prescribed and do it well. As Jeremiah Burroughs affirmed long ago, "In God's worship, there must be nothing tendered up to God but what He has commanded. Whatsoever we meddle with in the worship of God must be what we have a warrant for out of the Word of God."[5] The Scriptures have a lot to say about how we are to worship God. If we seek to please God in our worship, then we do well to seek to worship in the manner in which He has prescribed.

---

5 Jeremiah Burroughs, *Gospel Worship* (Morgan, PA: Soli Deo Gloria, 1990), 11.

Conclusion

In this book, I have endeavored to explain the nature, authority, purpose, and worship of the church. It is my hope that, along with gaining a better understanding of the nature of the church, we enjoy a greater appreciation and love for the church that leads us to be faithfully committed to serving and glorifying Christ in the church.

Review Questions

1. Why does the Bible regulate how we worship God?

2. Why must worship not be man centered?

3. Why must worship be Word centered?

4. Why is holiness vital in worship?

5. Why is worship to be spiritual?

6. Why must worship be orderly?

7. Why should singing be congregational?

8. What is the regulative principle of worship?

9. Why is the regulative principle important?

*Now to him who is able to do far more abundantly
than all that we ask or think,
according to the power at work within us,
to him be glory in the church and in Christ Jesus
throughout all generations, forever and ever. Amen*
Ephesians 3:20–21